A Methodology of Bi-Directional Data Transformation in Emerging Research and Opportunities

Kaleem Razzaq Malik
Muhammad Farhan
Noor Zaman Jhanjhi
Rana M. Amir Latif
Khalid Hussain
Syed Jawad Hussain

ELIVA PRESS

ELIVA PRESS

Kaleem Razzaq Malik
Muhammad Farhan
Noor Zaman Jhanjhi
Rana M. Amir Latif
Khalid Hussain
Syed Jawad Hussain

Relational Databases (RDBs) are largely employed, and so are often common as part of the car-rental age of software to both keep and retrieve information. RDBs are suitable to pay substantial data with no seeing about their semantics. Software dealing using RDB for information are conversant with this significance of information in their use from the system, but the semantics aren't a portion of their information version. The typical frame provided within just Semantic Web (SW) provides ability into those approaches to reuse and share information across diverse applications and platforms together side symbolizing their information connection - era. Since SW continues to be generated to your internet and progress, it has proven to be more invaluable in a variety of locations, especially if information from other sources must be exchanged or coordinated. It is not as achievable to displace all of the procedures data in the RDF sort, because most software continues to be related to RDB centered information representation. This dependence simplifies the notion of why both of those data units are essential to pay current tendency toward information storage and recovery. A methodology will become necessary since effective at altering data amongst RDB and RDF and storing data undamaged. This technique will turn out to be favorable to approaches at case concentrated or spread to utilize equally data units deprived of anxieties of shift. Hence such an approach can lower the conceptual difference amongst RDB along with RDF information units, leading to forming a concerted atmosphere such as advanced and traditional technologies along with the app. Most Information Regarding company-oriented approaches continues to be predicated around the relational data version. About the flip side, Semantic Internet statistics version RDF has come to be the newest benchmark for information modelling and investigation. As a result of the example integration of RDB and RDF information units has turned into the mandatory characteristic of these processes. This issue was a recent age scorching research issue. Many services, such as languages and tools, have been supplied in the form of Transformation of information out of RDB into RDF.

Published: Eliva Press SRL
Address: MD-2060, bd.Cuza-Voda, 1/4, of. 21 Chişinău, Republica
Moldova
Email: info@elivapress.com
Website: www.elivapress.com

ISBN: 978-1-952751-77-6

A METHODOLOGY OF BI-DIRECTIONAL DATA TRANSFORMATION IN EMERGING RESEARCH AND OPPORTUNITIES

[1]Kaleem Razzaq Malik
[2]Muhammad Farhan
[3]Noor Zaman Jhanjhi
[4]Rana M. Amir Latif
[5]Khalid Hussain
[6]Syed Jawad Hussain
krmalik@gmail.com[1]
farhansajid@gmail.com[2]
noorzaman.jhanjhi@taylors.edu.my[3]
ranaamir10611@gmail.com[4]
kusmani.utm@gmail.com[5]
Jawad@biit.edu.pk[6]

ABSTRACT

Relational Databases (RDBs) are largely employed, and so are often common as part of the car-rental age of software to both keep and retrieve information. RDBs are suitable to pay substantial data with no seeing about their semantics. Software dealing using RDB for information are conversant with this significance of information in their use from the system, but the semantics aren't a portion of their information version. The typical frame provided within just Semantic Web (SW) provides ability into those approaches to reuse and share information across diverse applications and platforms together side symbolizing their information connection - era. Since SW continues to be generated to your internet and progress, it has proven to be more invaluable in a variety of locations, especially if information from other sources must be exchanged or coordinated. It is not as achievable to displace all of the procedures data in the RDF sort, because most software continues to be related to RDB centered information representation. This dependence simplifies the notion of why both of those data units are essential to pay current tendency toward information storage and recovery. A methodology will become necessary since effective at altering data amongst RDB and RDF and storing data undamaged. This technique will turn out to be favorable to approaches at case concentrated or spread to utilize equally data units deprived of anxieties of shift. Hence such an approach can lower the conceptual difference amongst RDB along with RDF information units, leading to forming a concerted atmosphere such as advanced and traditional technologies along with the app. Most Information Regarding company-oriented approaches continues to be predicated around the relational data version. About the flip side, Semantic Internet statistics version RDF has come to be the newest benchmark for information modelling and investigation. As a result of the example integration of RDB and RDF information units has turned into the mandatory characteristic of these processes. This issue was a recent age scorching research issue. Many services, such as languages and tools, have been supplied in the form of Transformation of information out of RDB into RDF. These remedies tend not to insure to overcome most of the issues linked to the sleek use of information conversion attributes. This investigation tries to offer an essential method in covering information mapping, data conversion, and shift handle. Bidirectional data conversion working with a mutual language may encourage controlling shift and upgrade topics regarding information and metadata.

Keywords: *Relational Databases (RDBs), Semantic Web (SW), Extensible Markup Language (XML), Ontology Language (OWL), Relational Database Management System (RDBMS)*

2

Table of Contents

List of Figures

List of Tables

List of Abbreviations

SW	Semantic Web
RDF	Resource Description Framework
OWL	Ontology Language
XML	Extendable Markup Language
KDD	Knowledge Discovery Databases
SPARQL	SPARQL Protocol and RDF Query Language
RDFS	Description Framework Schema
RDBS	Relational Database Schema
DBMS	Database Management Systems

1 INTRODUCTION

1.1 Background

RDB Is now utilized as an industrial big data version for storage. Moreover, now, while the present fad is not precisely adapting to the proceed accessibility of information online where nearly all can be found using the internet and Cloud Computing. Thus, world-wide-web hardware, applications, and services are designed to be used whenever if they're near or much whenever demanded. If looking for the spread information has turned into a significant price while the craggy ratio of precisely wanted data can be seen. Thus, to eliminate this kind of crucial dilemma, Tim Berners-Lee, the father of internet engineering, created the notion of Semantic Web (SW) (Malik et al., 2018a). Currently, the development of the Internet from SW has been not yet been developed and entirely braced to its area of the world wide web since it had been designed to function as the principal notion of SW demanded the complete advancement from the science of world comprehensive web engineering. Berner Lee's vision was faked, just like a hopeless attempt to be both deployed and implemented. Moreover, it released a brand-new data version called Resource Description Framework (RDF) to get Semantic Internet. Semantic Web (SW) Arrived together with the notion of tools connecting using every other using circumstance and significance to produce Immediate presence In the Sphere of Web-based Information (Blue and Adler, 2001).

The area of study and concern over the last years has been collecting knowledge from link databases (RDB) open to this SW. In addition, many attempts have already been made to address the mapping and transfer of knowledge from the list of conventional yet continuing open technologies. Those structures, such as XML and RDB, are translated as RDF for the compilation of more detailed details. The most typical course of action is called "RDB-To-RDF" when data may be transferred to RDF or the set of encoding data using the aim it can challenge using the SPARQL Protocol and RDF Quarry Language (SPARQL). In September 2012, W3C launched a dialect and representative, as R2RML will symbolize an RDB mapping along with RDF data units to build instruments focused on that language. How-when mapping is involved, the R2RML is constrained. The bulk of up-to-date business-focused methods to data collection and retrieval are linked databases (RDBs). The improved field of organized online data is linked (Maamari et al., 2006).

The Semantic-web gives typical network licenses for cross-smart for program knowledge to be accessed and compacted. In diverse fields of concern, such technologies have been found useful in particular where knowledge may be shared or synchronized from various outlets. Semantic Net (SW), yet another development of the Internet, would grow tremendously. Older innovations have been turned into modern forms with the help of the latest technology update. And files developed with the

Extendable Markup Language (XML) have been enhanced for registration with the Semantic World Web. Triplets in this domain, predicate and origin are accessible online. Both these are often linked to hierarchically ordered outlets that use graphical representations. Internet Ontology Language (OWL) provides a semantically improved categorization of knowledge in order to generate certain forms of data that function only on various domain names, as well as problems. The final outcome is in RDF-like form. OWL seen, which can be sold across the world, as shown in Figure 1.

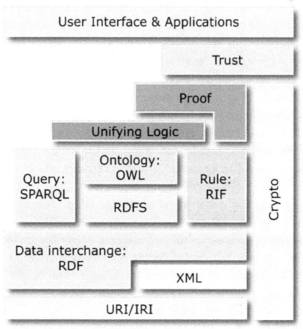

Figure 1Layered Structure of Web Semantics by W3C

Previously, various RDB-to-RDF approaches have been studied and several separate mappings from RDB-to-RDF have been drawn to the processes used to convert RDB and web-semantic metric units. These systems are confined to the synchronization of details and often establish a querying framework for SPARQL and knowledge connected to display the data because RDF. The strongest technique of group RDB-to-RDF interference is to discounted written access or update to this RDB or funding with any other knowledge access modalities. The key part of knowledge and details on the Site is accessed and used by all Relational Database Management System (RDBMS) (Steenkamp, 2017). This knowledge variant of the relations comprises of a relational database. The structures, constraints and organizational assistance of the knowledge system are characteristic. Transforming relational data into the data-centric Serial network version involves diligent mapping into models. Several protocols and tools are seen to aid by offering analysis methods for translation of partnership knowledge to harmonize with contemporary semantic techniques. Instead, the method of translation aims to convert two data units to the same representations. There are also difficulties in the usage of improved usability and consistency to achieve outcomes. Different scientists have sought various techniques to achieve the mandatory accomplishment of another worldwide century, Semantic Internet. Independent intelligence researchers have often succeeded by defining tools, and utilizing cutting-edge technologies, which includes the internet, to obtain more than the drawback and the necessary performance.

1.2 Motivation

Relational Databases (RDBs) are largely employed, and so are often common as part of the car-rental age of software to both keep and retrieve information. RDBs are suitable to pay substantial data with no seeing about their semantics. Software dealing using RDB for information are conversant with this significance of information in their use from the system, but the semantics aren't a portion of their information version. The typical frame provided within just Semantic Web (SW) provides ability into those approaches to reuse and share information across diverse applications and platforms together side symbolizing their information connection - era. Since SW continues to be generated to your internet and progress, it has proven to be more invaluable in a variety of locations, especially if information from other sources must be exchanged or coordinated. It is not as achievable to displace all of the procedures data in the RDF sort, because most software continues to be related to RDB centered information representation. This dependence simplifies the notion of why both of those data units are essential to pay current tendency toward information storage and recovery. A methodology will become necessary since effective at altering data amongst RDB and RDF and storing data undamaged. This technique will turn out to be favorable to approaches at case concentrated or spread to utilize equally data units deprived of anxieties of shift. Hence such an approach can lower the conceptual difference amongst RDB along with RDF information units, leading to forming a concerted atmosphere such as advanced and traditional technologies along with the app.

1.3 Problem Statement

Most Information Regarding company-oriented approaches continues to be predicated around the relational data version. About the flip side, Semantic Internet statistics version RDF has come to be the newest benchmark for information modelling and investigation. As a result of the example integration of RDB and RDF information units has turned into the mandatory characteristic of these processes. This issue was a recent age scorching research issue. Many services, such as languages and tools, have been supplied in the form of Transformation of information out of RDB into RDF. These remedies tend not to insure to overcome most of the issues linked to the sleek use of information conversion attributes. This investigation tries to offer an essential method in covering information mapping, data conversion, and shift handle. Bidirectional data conversion working with a mutual language may encourage controlling shift and upgrade topics regarding information and metadata.

1.4 The objective of the Study

The study was aimed at comparing and mapping instruments and transformation systems between RDB and the Web that are now available. This research would help to create more and more technology-based data extraction and storage systems, RDB and Semantic Internet. It aims to reduce the response time of DB inquiries and to improve connectivity with all internet knowledge and semantically improved details.

- Mapping Variances in schema and statistics amounts
- Enriching the DB contents to include semantics
- Pinpointing grey regions in developed languages and tools such as transformation involving RDB and RDF
- Production of calculations along with their execution
- Assessing alternative place at the finish RDB and RDF to stage outside that the shift trigger

1.5 Transformation Methodology

Research of now offered tools and methods together side their frameworks used as a condition of their art to get a conversion. Subsequently, find feeble locations along with providing a different mechanism to change. For bidirectional conversion to get the job done nicely, we have certainly to map diverse schema degree transformations. In this exploration, we'll look profoundly into obtainable mappings, implementations, and upgrades just as for every needed using a few cases to try our effects. By doing this, we'll produce calculations, tables, and instances to achieve desirable benefits. Afterwards, these consequences will probably be examined and discussed dependent upon the prior outcomes, as shown in Figure 2.

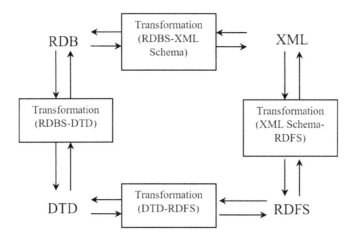

Figure 2 Complete Process of Bidirectional Transformation using different approaches like DTD and XML Schema

In Figure 3, the suggested methodology for this challenge is symbolized by mapping gaps in schema and statistics degree, accentuating the DB contents, differentiating grey locations, and the creation of calculations together side their execution. Delay variables in data recovery and storage systems might be made better by the induction of bidirectional transformation amid RDB and RDF schemas (Andersen et al., 2005).

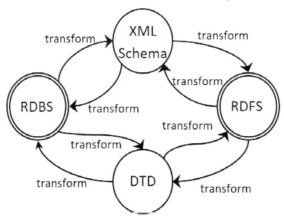

Figure 3 State Transition Diagram of Bidirectional Transformation using different approaches like DTD and XML

We reveal two stats since the end and starting up exist at the practice of information trans- creation amongst RDFS and RDB Schema accompanied closely by DTD or

XML Schema. The bidirectional transformation back and from into RDB utilizing XML as intermediate statistics sort. Information and metadata throughout the conversion period shouldn't have lost while in the changeover in 1 sort into the next. Afterwards, by dispersing shared data sets XML, acquired throughout the straight back, and on data conversion practice, the discovery of the big change in data or metadata calls for to be quantified. With all these dimensions, counter pruning jobs should have work to earn change achievable by upgrading the RDF retail store or RDB, just where it's necessary (Rouse et al., 2011).

1.6 Data Models

An information model is an abstraction to Be a Symbol of information, together with its limitations, abilities, and power. This informative article majorly centers on just three data units that are RDB, XML, and RDF.

1.6.1 Relational Database (RDB)

A connection in RDB is buildup Over a mix of columns and rows in which each cell reflects one parcel of data labelled underneath a field. An area makes up about a column, along with the arrow, reflects a good example of recording regarding the latest relation in an area desk. The information version of RDB can be a mix of this data sort, restriction, and operational dependence on the information (Bindu et al., 2019). Information with regards to just about every part of information contrary to a connection is retained in the shape of the schema (construction characterized for the information to be kept in a connection) and information worth (precise literals saved at desk cells). On the internet, RDB can be utilized in the back end for the storage of information.

1.6.2 Extensible Markup Language (XML)

Inventions such as the net in media levied the necessity of intermediate terminology that may create data-backed among all of the procedures attached close by. Which also attracted the production of XML within an intermediate speech. It turned into a common language immediately after 0s and 1s pieces that can be near into a system using high-frequency comprehension and translation, utilized as machine-processable terminology. Service of information types one of RDB, XML, and RDF throughout mapping engage in with an essential job when seeking to alter one's information version into the following. Customization of information types are potential in XML Schema (XML) (Andersen et al., 2001).

The format That's Called XML record provides the internet with tags that include structured user-determined and classified marks. However, to modify the relation schema to RDF, we have to do it as an XML system, after which the RDF schema is linked to XML, or DTD to RDF schema. In addition, it then transforms into the first schema form.

If XML is essential, it can be used normally for software, equipment, and computers to provide a standard for the conversion of your data. The vocabulary based on XML and XML is publicly flexible with more persons for your net, because HTML concepts promote your data in virtually every other platform sponsored by the electric system. Customization can allow the centralized access to knowledge highly useful summary. Nearly any wise system now promotes XML. This service may be the key explanation why XML has become a common and well-known format for worldwide database communications. In comparison, a database is less organized and semi-structured because hunting data is nuanced and far less precise (Stanslaski et al., 2009).

1.6.3 Resource Description Framework (RDF)

On the internet, for hunting and obtaining sources such as individuals, videos, etc. Audios, graphics, etc. on hunt motors serve like something online. Despite slow progress introduced into such internet search engines like google, a more dramatic rise in the level of world-wide-web content generates a reduction in technological advances. To fix this dilemma world wide web content representation must become altered to processable server structure. Semantic Web (SW) has released server processable kind with all the assistance of all Resource Description Framework (RDF) (Loprinzi et al., 2013). Following donations are significant in the Area of Information transformation involving RDB and RDF:

- Mapping of Distinct information units along with their personalization
- Four RDB schema formulas in XML schema transformation algorithm, XML schema to RDF schema algorithm, RDF schemes in XML Schema transformation algorithm and XML Schema to RDB Schemas transformation algorithms in the construct schema
- Four calculations RDB into XML Transformation Algorithm, XML into RDF Trans- creation Algorithm, RDF into XML Transformation XML, also XML into RDB Transformation Algorithm on assembling information through Bidirectional conversion procedure
- Released a version Bidirectional Information Transformation Product (BDTM) to get bi-directional data conversion
- The execution revealing BDTM established conversion strategy of Info
- Resolution to upgrade difficulty for That information discovered in the two kinds RDB and also RDF

1.7 Socio-Economic and Other Benefits of data Transformation

After points signify distinct socioeconomic Added Benefits With the assistance of suggested methodology:

- Racking wide-ranging information dispersed on the web using rapid and efficient recovery and storage
- Integrating RDBs of those approaches predicated on considerable, dispersed, and data that is disgusting.
- Adding RDBs from Other platform Are a Lot More expensive and intricate
- Proposed methodology enhances functioning in either data wide-ranging or bright surroundings observed in RDF-based information merchants underneath the spreading character of this strategy.
- The methodology, even once employed, will specifically gain technique comprising traditional and semantic-enriched data-storage.
- This strategy will soon start fresh chances for research and projects to work in an Academic and expert degree.
- The method may end up being quite a stunning advancement together with the improved use and compatibility one of platform regarding semantic net by departing the region of the machine, perhaps not mandatory necessitates upgrades for Pakistan businesses to become fascinated.
- The plan helps to cause enormous scale loss-less conversion of the conventional approaches to semantically improved systems forth and back. Data conversion may improve yield on investments.
- Enriched compatibility with programs with semantic or information data model may reward Us to proceed 1 step ahead of forthcoming fashion of internet-based techniques.

2 HETEROGENEITY IN DATA

2.1 Overview

The World Wide Web (WWW) allows general people to extend the information from enormous database storehouses world-wide. A step of information grows loads of databases. It's crucial to seek out at the information to clinic apparatus for far better understood mega net searcher. That was just a significant part of world wide web indicators and directories reachable now, re-covering substantial information is bothersome. But to overcome the dilemma from the world wide web, telltale web improvements are supposing an outstanding component. It's hugely hard for world-wide web-oriented software to successfully come-up using an effective system to form out information and also to understand how to investigate the large details (McBrien and Poulovassilis, 2003). This portion ponders the institution of enormous data recovery with conversion mechanics utilizing query-oriented systems or platforms, wherever data units have been considered crucial components for organizing data and information contacts are all employed to talk into this Wrong connection among information companies. A couple of different forms of concerns regarding this apparatus are likewise researched, that isn't the exact very same as queries regarding traditional societal networking (Foster et al., 2005).

It's much less Demanding to earn advice compared to explore information. The burst of advice will soon turn to a substantial dilemma of information representation. Without proficient and viable investigation mechanics, it will probably be underwater via this unique step of advice. By the standpoint of gear, dispersed calculating and also crucial appropriated inventions would be the possible replies for enormous advice; otherwise, by the perspective of applications, many mining advancements have been intended and intended to maintain functioning onto a self-indulgent framework (Okunseinde and Stading, 2010). From the conditions of tremendous info, it's verging on confident most expertise Knowledge Discovery Databases (KDD) obtainable now & most ordinary mining calculations are unable to be attached straightforwardly to organize the expansive amount of advice. Generally, both pre-processing tracking about the grounds of both KDD and perhaps the information mining advancements needs to be upgraded for Internet monitoring systems, which may supply a lot of facts. Semantic web-based systems, in addition to frequent representation, might be used under consideration to solve substantial information retrieval (AlBahar and Huang, 2019).

Different Scientists have tried distinct methods to match the compulsory results for attaining to another generation net between semantics and statistics linkage. You've been efforts for altering database schema to Extensible Markup Language Schema (XMLS) or Document Type Definition (DTD) or source Description Framework Schema (RDFS) possibly completely or partially. Likewise, the reverse conversion might be achieved by DTD to the database schema. DTDs by the ending of the XML record to your web might be altered and merged into RDF schema. By studying labels in XML record, we can select one of them suiting to your fulfilling job regarding property or class. About the flip side, the XML record is upgraded to obtain the capability to be translated as RDF. It'd be safer if XML's unique arrangement stays unchanged throughout the conversion procedure for a much better outcome and better policy (Malik et al., 2018a).

What's more, the transformation may happen out of DTD into OWL-based Ontology as an advanced format. In detail, the notion of tools connecting one of data-base, DTD, XML, and RDF with inquiries without altering the context and significance of data that is online to make its organizational presence. These procedures might be obtained to receive a single-side conversion strategy.

Most of the Information And data are observed online and are saved and recovered utilizing RDBs. Just work in different search indicates which Semantic Internet cooperation, along with different domain names, expands its usage over and above the internet (Singh et al., 2012). Several procedures and applications are released to assist with supplying means to research information data representations to its access to semantic-web based techniques. There are still issues in attaining results using higher compatibility and performance.

Database schemas and ontologies always evolve to satisfy your shifting user and application requirements. Hence, based mappings involving your two needs to also evolve, so rather than being calmed or re-discovered out of scratch. Update for information has been altered continues to be under development, and its semantics isn't yet properly described; there is some vagueness about the transformation of a SPARQL update statements. Moreover, just fundamental (relation-to-class along with attribute-to-property) mappings are researched thus far. The dilemma of upgrading relational information by way of SPARQL update is like the traditional database perspective upgrade dilemma, hence delivering proposed solutions could contribute greatly in addressing this specific situation (Pon et al., 2002).

2.2 Background

A greater era of intelligence discovery is known as science fiction. It includes the concept of data gathering, processing and assessment through numerous methods of computational, methodology and scientific modeling and application, such as data mining, mathematical analysis, data bases, learning, pattern recognition and visualization. Data engineering work is currently well tailored to rich computational techniques in order to obtain better data information from thickness and thickness analysis on detail creation, data processing, statistical modelling, mathematical modeling, computer learning and artificial intelligence (Iftikhar and Pedersen, 2011).

Information processing and predictive testing have been a critical feature of data science exploration and have become a new sphere of study at the latest. The great majority of the related work has been located in the broad data field (Latif et al., 2019a). The Majority of the Information discovered now is Stored in Relational databases. The relational database Consists of a hierarchical information version. Just about every relation at a DB is represented in a tabular format, which follows regulations of the hierarchical information version. Most of the information and advice that have been observed online can be saved and recovered utilizing RDBs (Tallat et al., 2019). The previous investigation indicates that Semantic Internet cooperation, along with different domain names, expands its usage past the internet. Several procedures and applications are released to assist by delivering the techniques to research information data for accessibility to Semantic Internet software. Nonetheless, there are still issues in certainly gaining results using higher compatibility and performance. Various scientists have tried distinct methods to accomplish the compulsory upshot of attaining another generation world-wide-web, which can certainly be the Semantic Internet (Aldabbas et al., 2020).

The Semantic Net (SW) may be used for the Internet, allowing so many different terms understood by people and PCs to view knowledge. Knowledge concerning SW has been seen using the second online model, defined as the Definition Source Structure (Latif et al., 2019c) (RDF). Philosophy can be an important aspect of a few of the ideas used as a portion of the SW base, and even of the RDFS, as well as the OWL (Ontology Languages Internet) are the two W3C advised chemicals that interact with ontologies. Even the SW will improve more qualified transparency, roboticist, mediation and reuse guidance and include support for interoperability problems not subject to existing net change. At this moment, the analysis of the semantic-network indicators is another issue earlier and the new ecosystems of world-wide Network indicators are demolished by conventional search services as for e.g., Yahoo, Google, and Bing (Latif et al., 2020).

The analysis includes Exhibited about the internet statistics conversion to extract carefully related information. In the current period of semantical annotation breakthroughs, there's the various grade of information data units, software, and sorts of data rendering and processes of related databased communicating. Each of the designs was custom-made for certain undertakings and aims. The endurance of conventions and standards may be made better at a societal platform by shooting in outcomes from alerting operators at continuous and genuine during the next justification regulations generated by ontologies. Ontologies are discussed by unique dialects in telltale net moving from source Description Framework Schema (RDFS) that will be weakest into Internet Ontology Language (OWL) that could be the very seated (Ramzan et al., 2019).

We cannot state nevertheless That telltale net invention is deemed mature and complete to become confessed with industry on a grand scale. A few of the versions need adjustments and fitting tool aid. Yet soaring mechanical aspects think about, e.g., gears, variants, college, administrations for conditional assessing, Un-Attended diagnostics and upkeep, etc. on for always a certain useful resource of internet resources. Such resources are innovative, aside from the view of changing qualities to get a couple also attributes from your view of evolving "status-marks" (condition of their advantage). Present RDF even now necessitates passing and plausible augmentations (Latif et al., 2019b).

Law enforcement officers should be able to identify and evaluate the modus operandi of the illegal activity, in order to recognize the inter-connections between suspects. We also studied group identification using the graph theory of crime networks and have formally developed a modern method for detecting groups. The approach encourages law enforcement authorities to analyze and therefore take a broader perspective of the crime network. We view this as an option or extension to the above-mentioned methods of mutual identification. The algorithm suggested enables the identification of multiple systems and behaviors in the same group and assists them (Sangkaran et al., 2020a).

The report focuses on an evaluation of the probability of accident by artificial intelligence augmented by road vehicles. The probability of collision is estimated to be 3.52 times higher in one direction and 77% lower. In other cases, the chance is 2.95 times larger. The report estimated the probability of a road haulage accident at railway crossings to be reduced to 85%. It can contribute to the creation of an automated railway crossing collision avoidance scheme (Singhal et al., 2020).

Air quality and health applications are developed and enhanced through software engineers. When Air Quality Monitoring (AQM) stations are clustered in metropolitan environments, residential address or any place becomes a spatial concern. In this analysis, we propose to find the locations of health info, and measure distances with AQM stations, a 4-part Space Engineering Algorithm. The algorithm would connect health records to the nearest AQM station so that air emissions can be the. In Klang Valley, Malaysia, the proposed algorithm is used as a case study. The findings indicate that the algorithm suggested will effectively produce health data for air emissions (Usmani et al., 2020).

Ransomware encrypts the data of the attackers or locks the system's users out. Petya targets people and businesses through email attachments and links for download. NotPetya has worms and abuses the weaknesses of EternalBlue and EternalRomance. Three-Level Authentication is a ransomware approach that uses virtual machines and window extensions to search all files that the consumer needs to import from Internet (Ren et al., 2020).

Analysis of crime networks has gained numbers as network monitoring has become more commonplace. In this review, the group identification methods based on graph analysis have been thoroughly examined. Further research is required and planned to develop this field further, the study says. The definition of a population and algorithms for group identification in a network is specifically explored (Sangkaran et al., 2020b). In this remark, the functionality for the IT issue audit framework program is being checked. The purpose of this analysis is to determine the statistical value of consumer monitoring and service satisfaction. It also attempts to evaluate the statistically significant influence of consumer grievances on the level of service and to determine the effects of quality of service on customer engagement (Saeed et al., 2020a).

The authors review data mining techniques for calculation of high temperature, precipitation, loss and wind speed. This was achieved with vector assist profiles, decision-making tree, and weather data from 2015 and 2019 in Pakistan. The findings suggest that ample case knowledge may be used to quantify the atmosphere and environmental change it focuses on utilizing data mining techniques (Saeed et al., 2020b).

The IoT revolutionizes diverse industries, including hospitals, security, industry and more. This sophisticated technology, though, also at the same time triggered important safety problems. IoT networks remain susceptible to security breaches when 'people' are increasingly linked. The problem of unsafe routing on these IoT devices has become critical. There has been no detection or mitigation method which covers rank and wormhole attacks when initiated simultaneously on an IoT network. This research aims to lead to high efficiency and productive systems design and development (Jhanjhi et al., 2019).

Ransomware is created to rob the recipient with a ransom. At this point, early identification is essential to deter the attack from achieving its target. Machine learning is suggested before it begins its encryption feature, to identify crypto-ransomware. This method was extended to ensure that established and unknown crypto ransomware is identified more thoroughly. However, the use of a pre-encryption detection algorithm (PEDA) which consists of two phases will result in a high false positive rate (FPR). A Windows API created by a suspicious program could be caught and analyzed in the PEDA-Phase I. A suspect software was developed by PEDA and placed in a Step II signature repository. The two steps in PEDA culminated in two levels of crypto-ransomware early detection to guarantee the consumer has no missing data at all. This method can only detect established crypto-ransomware and it was precise and simple, albeit very rigid. In contrast with Naïve Bayes, Random Tree, Ensemble and EldeRan, LA had the lowest FPR at 1.56 percent (Kok et al., 2019).

Recently, data mining technologies concentrate on data mining decision tree classification approaches. Researchers was categorized into gender-relating therapies for lung cancer utilizing various clinical approaches and data sets for different age ranges. The age range (30-60 years) is contrasted to men and women with groups. The Rattle R and Weka instruments determine the best treatment method by-party for the study of a suitable treatment system. The two algorithms of the decision tree were then equivalent to 200 actual data sets in terms of classification accuracy (Saeed et al., 2019).

2.2.1 Semantic Annotation

At This Time, two or three smart web indicators have been written and actualized for assorted workplaces, and those parts that know those web-crawlers are somewhat special. This exploration includes a combined portrayal justification sub-par frame and higher-level library cosmology to complete a smart search instrument. By engine tool, demonstrating asks along with also an equation appraising present linked invention of the will handle and progress the growth of internet crawler, and specifying the asks of comprehension web-crawler.

The telltale net Enables PCs to grasp that the significance and semantics of their data obtainable around the internet. Even the semantics have profited the examination of linking, pursuit, and analysis of advice. The Connected advice is talked into by coordinated or semi-organized ontologies and can be represented by dialects, in special, source Description Framework (RDF), and world wide web doctrine dialect such as OWL. Even a metaphysics can be a formal special of this conceptualization. The notion is talked about utilizing properties and classes and connections one of these. The lessons are of many different forms, namely, subclass, superclass, convergence category, marriage category, along with the nutritional supplement category. These possessions will be mainly of two kinds, particularly information land and specific real estate. When altering data, version one type into prescriptive data version at RDF or OWL should encourage mapping between your two designs.

2.2.2 Data Transformation

Within the Previous decade, both with connections and symmetries in probabilistic units are proven to become incredibly capable of focusing on wide-ranging scale advice mining problems. Some of the many major surgeries in those raised methods are numbering, be it to get parameter/structure instruction for the skilled deduction. Commonly, none the less they only assess misusing the coherent arrangement making use of impromptu directors. This paper investigates whether a build-up of Graph Databases can be a feasible method of scaling augmented probabilistic derivation and mastering plans. We demonstrate the graph database query to find both equally proper and surmised amounts might create leading border derivation and finding out approaches asks of scope quicker, without generating implementation.

2.2.3 Data Extraction

Data retrieval Via looking for information around the internet isn't just a clear idea but instead includes identifying difficulties if it's contrasted with overall data retrieval. Diverse world-wide-web indicators yield identifying list goods on account of the number in search and search procedure. Google, Yahoo, and Bing are outside there that manages the questions while in the aftermath of organizing that the catchphrases. They simply query information is awarded about the site page, so because lately, a few mining parties start communicating results out of their semantics established on the search programs, also, but the increased portion of these come in their introductory phases. Till not one of the internet crawlers return to closing indexing on the entire website content, even a fantastic bargain less whole internet. Present internet could be your most economical global database that will not need the current presence of the semantic arrangement, and consequently, it makes to become problematic to your system to realize further that the information given by your customer as search strings.

2.3 Data Models Evolution History

This collection of links is defined by the Relational Database (RDB), formed in a hierarchy for the storage from file form for all incidents with fields defining details for containing link features. A standard developed generalized marking language (SGML) may be an Internet-oriented syntax built on a subset. A succinct XML archive of knowledge entity used for the actions of the program. Source Definition System (RDF) incorporates knowledge merger and linking functionality that use semantics to allow additional content to be exchanged and vulnerable. Construction Query Language (SQL) may be a question-language for the basic function of data collection, scanning, monitoring and exploitation. SPARQL Protocol and Query Language (SPARQL) may be used by RDF to search the data language as a query language. XML Route Language (XPath) is an XML navigational query language that says to pick nodes and then calculates the meaning in the XML file. Network Ontology Language (OWL) defines the expression with the capacity of transmitting constraint, a category of information and the structure and readability of the method. Total time-wise background of these information units such as RDB, XML, and RDF along using a contrast of communicating platforms and tools have been introduced in Figure 4 Subsequent, within this section, just about every statistics version's history will be symbolized by one.

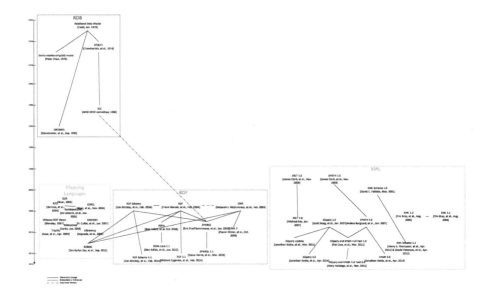

Figure 4 Complete history evolution concerning tools and data models for the transformation process

2.3.1 Relational Database (RDB)

Database Centered Data could maintain the shape of the normalized or non-normalized sort. As soon as we discuss non-normalized sort, then it truly is all about information saved in No SQL. About the flip side, hierarchical format worried mostly having a tabular type of information storage. One of the well-known SQL established database management system (DBMS) is popularly called MongoDB. But you'll find several relational database management techniques such as MySQL, Oracle, etc., used to saved information in data format. RDB information version was introduced, whereas querying a relational version predicated information was named as SEQUEL and has been suggested by Chamberlain. SEQUEL afterwards was called since SQL and manufactured that a common by ANSI committee in 1986. The development of historical past made information care and direction far more effective and potent.

Initially the relational system form was built utilizing the word "relational database" F. In 1970, IBM codded down. In comparison, Codd had 12 regulations to enforce the quality-data variant, named Codd's guidance, while Codd had a respected partnership within his paper "A Relational Data Model for Broad Collaborative Data Banks." These regulations have been introduced, albeit to the minimal and necessary standard, in setting up an internet desk and operators used to handle the data form. Initially it was named a SEQUEL and was usually built with SQL (Structured Query Language) on the ANSI X3H2 commission in 1986. In 1976 a template variant for Peter Chan's

26

encoding of knowledge for a linked agency type. The Stonebreaker Manifesto, which in 1996 became ORDBMS (Objective Relational Database Technical) in 1990, was the first to be introduced in the third development software framework. Time-wise description of data associated with RDB information version history development has been awarded at Table 1 Additional record of RDB is worried regarding the direct approach of this model.

Table 1: Historical Evolution of RDB

No.	Year	Author	Description	Key Term
1	Jun. 1970	[Codd, Jun. 1970]	A Relational Model for Large Shared Databanks	Relational Data-Model
2	1974	[Chamberlain, et al., 1974]	SEQUEL: A Structured English Query Language	SEQUEL
3	1976	[Peter Chen, 1976]	The entity-relationship model toward a unified view of data	Entity-relationship (ER) model
4	1986	[ANSI X3H2 committee, 1986]	Became an ANSI standard	SQL
5	Sep. 1990	[Stonebraker, et al., Sep. 1990]	Third-generation Database System Manifesto	ORDBMS

In Figure 5, we are linking them based on this deadline in the medial side to reveal their birth in line with this real history utilizing author and year facts. Currently, the next element test of XML has been symbolized.

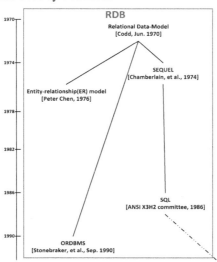

Figure 5 Evolution of RDB data and querying model

27

2.3.2 Extensible Markup Language (XML)

The arrangement of the Internet page will be Followed with W3C regulations constructed in XML. XML gets got the ability to present tailored tags readable using a system for more use in just about any type of app. XML is currently utilized like a common and standard vocabulary when altering data in 1 thing to the other from the area of science fiction. This thing may be a device, program, embedded applications, and online resources and solutions.

2.3.3 Data Models

Let us research variants of information units beginning from Normal into probably the newest statistics form utilized from the market of information sciences. This phase, we'll try to present information units such as Relational Information Product, Extensible Markup Language, Reference Growth Framework, World Wide Web Ontology Language, and JSON. None of the said data units is believed extent as an alternative. Their usage is rising swiftly: RDB, XML, RDF, OWL, and JSON.

3 BI-DIRECTIONAL DATA TRANSFORMATION

3.1 Overview

Conventional data methods majorly assemble upon a hierarchical information version, and the latest systems such as big data, cloud computing systems, and other relevant technologies established approaches, that can be using an information version to get progress in data linkage and rationale. Additionally, third party web-based systems possess the convenience of improved collaboration and communicating mechanism predicated on information compatibility together with intellect. There is a necessity to boost the information conversion mechanism to create the information usable to the kinds of techniques. It'd be more suitable to present a more bidirectional transformation on the list of information units to fix compatibility problems. In this analysis, information conversion between Relational Database Schema (RDBS) and Resource Description Framework Schema (RDFS) to his or her data arrangement capacities and information retention. The following procedure is even more broken up to mapping and even changing to many suitable choices that can be observed in every single information unit (Rozin and Kaplun, 1998). Extensible Markup Language (XML) is shared terminology, that plays with the vital purpose in the intermediate degree to get data conversion for information support along with foreseeing alter. Thus, bi-directional information Transformation product (BDTM) concentrate is really on transformation to regain far better outcomes in the sorts of both schemata plus also a frequent representation such as XML (Hongwei et al., 2003).

This study paper is additionally Organized and separated into six segments. The following portion covers information conversion linked literature. Afterwards, your section concerning the suggested version for bidirectional conversion mechanics has been symbolized. Then execution instalment predicated on data and algorithms form mapping looks comprising crucial information to ensure conversion-related. In the past, segments covering exclusive occasion analysis, outcome, disagreements, and judgment are all comprised.

3.2 Introduction

Significance of Information Within This age is Well recognized. The information is currently utilized to extract practical info, and it can be utilized to acquire wisdom regarding forecasting data statistics for its results assessing. The following procedure is set up by amassing information on the true-life events, organization events, organizational day to day activities along with their customs, and politics throughout us. Quantifiable advice tends to make statistics potential to link and assess several classes to data investigation. But, it's perhaps not a simple job to connect data since they're made up of distinct data units. Each information version has its very capability, limitations, and restrictions. A platform, just like the internet, demands upgrades to turn into effective working with any data stored from several sources such as apparatus, detectors, system, and different procedures. Just about every data version is required to map together with the other's data version at an architecture degree (Zhao et al., 2017). This mapping simplifies the key problems that can be faced in regards to supporting the conversion of information in data products to some other. Technically that this arrangement has been stored being metadata (data information) at an identical process. Thus, the moment the transformation occurs, then it will become essential to make use of or ship data and metadata collectively to continue mapping with no lack of advice. Additionally, this enhances the possibility of success speed the moment it has to do with assessing info's authentic temperament (Ebert, 2006).

The Internet Has Turned into the Potent Resource of information travel in One Set into the next. The information must be to be saved, controlled, recovered, and upgraded with using efficient and specialized mechanics. These mechanics are needed to grow enough to deal with a top degree of information sophistication and dependence. This maturity data might be done; lots of Database Management Systems (DBMS) have been launched and utilized by ten years or so. Every one of that DBMS abides by a kind of information version for storage and recovery. Whereas a data version will function as included of information buildings, limitations, and surgeries that are employed into a kind of information. Databases are derived from community, Relational, Hierarchal, and item information units, which can be utilized for information representation data storage and direction. The information has a lot of contours; however, in the data product, a connection will be represented utilizing a kind of table with columns and rows (Kotob, 1987). Each case comes from row portion, although most of the features seeing a thing to whom table goes out on columns. In data, version limitations are all predicated on ethics, cardinality, and restriction, etc. At that purpose of operational support, they are starting up out of production to alteration together side regulations of normalization so you can get improved effects. The supply of information might be contingent on the necessity if it contributes to normalization or even de-normalization. As talked about early in the day, web-data can be situated in the shape of the relational database. This information will be moved into the proper execution Extensible Markup Language (XML) if required by infantry programs and software. Currently, finding its way towards web technological innovation at which XML manufactured its markers for moving information independent of application and platform used as a frequent terminology. Data transformation and translation happens to utilize XML as an intermediate kind of information. For utilizing the personalization for the maximum capacity, information is subsequently invisibly to a schema with data predicated arrangement (Callow and Kalawsky, 2013).

Even the Chief way to obtain web-data stems in societal networking, existence and statistics mediums software preserved using direction platform to get Relational Databases. Data conversion has turned into a hard endeavor amongst two data units. These version limits and benefits can get beneath the manner of conversion procedure when involved in data correctness and completeness. An attentive mechanism must attain far better consequences for mapping both the data units to ensure all of the advice with no reduction. This mapping can ensure all potential problems regarding construction, limitations, and procedures help. Data units such as RDB, XML, and source Description Framework (RDF) are built to encourage very different reasons like connections, commonness, and statistics linkage centered systems that are separate. Data version predicated on RDB handles advice relationships while preserving them recognizable. Whereas, XML is a markup language established data version utilized to extend a top degree of personalization and typical kind of information representation. At length, the RDF-based information version is sold from the shape of related information keeping undamaged traceability and link attached with every portion of their data used (Sabornie et al., 1988).

Both XML and RDF elegance provide the whole application creation capabilities and functionality. XML Provides the support of components along with building and container capacity to be shared with ordinary, harmonious and transparent machines and applications. Mathematically constructed on XML technologies, the RDF-based knowledge is further improved by the development of connections with uniqueness and a hierarchical connection named knowledge connect. Both XML and RDF may be used to pay for some type of details for distribution and acceptance with increased accuracy and precision opportunities. In comparison to the kind of knowledge provided on the semantic web, OWL may find it complicated to pay for the knowledge in its entirety exactly. In order for the two knowledge retrieval disciplines (RDBMS) and semi-enriched (Semantic Web) to overcome vulnerabilities, an informatic bi-directional transformation technique has been supplied. If a change would not affect the ingenuity of this material, it will be altered. However, the monitoring of enormous data would often become an opportunity for a quick and efficient approach (Zhou and Ho, 2007). It will allow the knowledge and intellectual extension work. Such an ecosystem is capable of translating knowledge structures, such as their reliability and interoperability, into the spreading nature of such procedures, as shown in Figure 6.

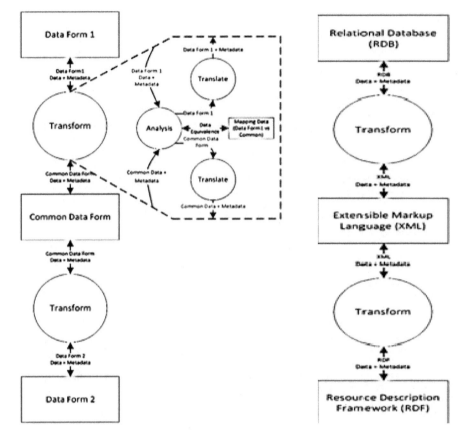

Figure 6 Proposed Model and Generic Level Representation

3.3 Bidirectional Data Transformation Model (BDTM)

Means of information conversion in All facets by claiming reduction to less is tricky but not difficult to attain. Must essential requirement always be to assess the accessibility of communicating mechanics attentively, to turn into in a position in building fresh one if noncompliance with conversion course of action to finish? To reach similar capacities proposed version has been introduced with XML as an intermediate degree of the information conversion procedure. The version of this suggested bi-directional conversion procedure is represented, revealing transformation-taking spots involving RDB and RDF, as exhibited in Fig. Whereas, XML is required arriving involving of their both conversion of information is out of RDB into RDF or even RDF into RDB. This version additionally implements the process itself is build-up on translation, mapping, and conversion algorithms or mechanisms. Mapping is superbly performed between statistics units of RDB, RDF, and XML. These statistics units ensure limitations in data, datatypes, as well as data arrangements. The navigation mechanism handles solution into each information representative at additional abbreviated terminology if it goes back to XML, RDB, or even RDF. Transformation is the procedure of reforming information removed out of data products, as shown in Figure 7.

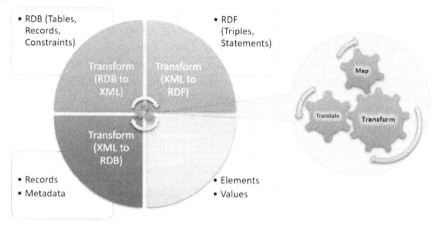

Figure 7 Abstract Model representing Bidirectional Transformation Process

Crucial Actions in the Procedure for transformation out of a single Data form to any kind:

- Formulated a container information version before beginning a transformation
- Know All Potential limitations that Must be recorded
- Build a strategy the Way to incorporate Two programs, e.g., D B and XML or even XML and RDF
- Devise resolutions into the problems appearing because of compatibilities and constraints
- Generate Your remedy to overcome this difficulty
- Validation of every conversion
- Take good care of outcomes by getting Ready to Additional procedure based on this proposed version
- Backward transformation is essential in the event of two paradigms

Information extraction out of RDB Is Finished Utilizing SQL dependent questions. Whereas information extraction at the event there is an RDF retail store afterwards, SPARQL symbolizes the query platform very similar to SQL out of RDF. The forwards or backward information ingestion necessitates SQL just in the case there is RDB and also SPARQL just in the event of RDF. Afterwards, both of those information extraction carries meta-data as well as turn into effective of shifting from 1 sort into the next, which in our instance is RDB or even RDF. Right after extraction is more total, then translation and mapping of information Start-S for XML information version. With all the entire crucial advice accumulated for conversion, to begin with, then information and metadata both have been altered and save to two individual data files. Data right after conversion has been stored right into an XML document using expansion XML, whereas even metadata or advice concerning data arrangement is saved from the XML Schema document using extension XSD. Later, the transformation would always be to hit upon destination data structure, and it will be RDB if forwards conversion and RDF in the event of inverse conversion, as shown in Figure 8.

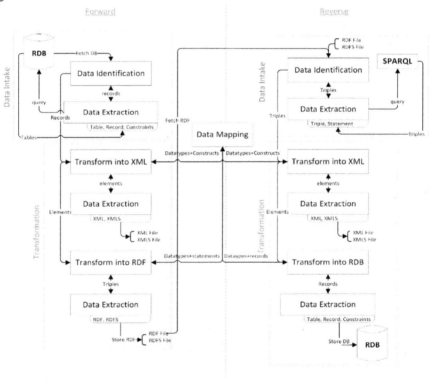

Figure 8 Bidirectional Transformation Model for forwarding and Reverse Process Execution of the data

Today It's Time to Spell out the way to call XML rather than Direct transformation. In reply to the question could be your requirement for keeping an eye on a modification that could be the critical portion with the full process creation. XML gets to be quite a frequent port of information in catching shift source. Thus, in service to assess whether the shift was bought in the opposite of this bi-directional conversion procedure. Subsequently, it might encourage calculation required to detect and alter influence affect RDB.

3.3.1 Datatype Mapping

It Is Crucial to map present representation One of Cervical schema, DTD, XML Schema, along with RDFS. For that reason, we've utilized a tabular representation in Table 2 to reveal the corresponding Schema thing for its every notion of this hosting. All these things have been used for good transformation in between RDB and telltale net.

Table 2: Syntax and Semantic Comparison of RDB and RDF data models

Term	Relational Schema	XML Schema	RDFS
Table	Table_Name	Complex type element	Class
Field	Field_Name	Element	Rdf: Property
Cardinality	Field (>=0)	Restriction (Pattern)	owl:restriction
Cardinality	Field (>0)	Restriction (Pattern)	owl:restriction
Referencing	Field	Simple type element Ref xs: keyref	domain (Property)
Primary Key	Field	xs: key	Range (Property)
Composite key	Fields	xs: key	Rdfs:subPropertyOf
Data type	Field	Type	Type

3.3.2 Cases Involved

Once in two phases, instances of transition from RDB into XML, XML into RDFS are concerned about all the meaning, while each case is focused on the two symbols or keywords, which involve mapping things together, whether they appear like as they are meant to be doing during analysis.
RDB Schema to XML Schema

- Characteristic in XML Schema may be Utilized to Be a Symbol of the main key of this table to get RDB compelling Unique-ness during usage = "Expected."
- Uncomplicated element with the ref as it pertains to a different ingredient is symbolizing a mention secret to another connection.
- The sequence in complicated component reflects different aspects of RDB Table Where-as table has been represented with the component Alone
- When aspects are put in the parenthesis, could be one split by comma signifies are a subconscious child of their parent node ingredient.
- But variety as an instance xs = "series" at XML Schema is symbolizing the exact data type of this field that in cases like this could simply be varChar without having to reveal that the period of this discipline in RDB (that may be solved with design characterized for applicable area variety).

3.4 Introduction

- Analyzing data
- Data mapping
- Data transformation

3.5 Algorithms

We could proceed ahead of the execution department because the Needed information linked to the technology used is increasingly being introduced up to needed degree of depth, as shown in Figure 9.

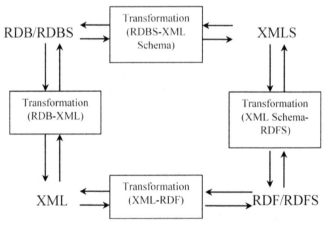

Figure 9 Diagram of Algorithms with Inputs and Outputs

3.5.1 Schema Transformation Algorithms

Algorithm: Transformation from RDBS to XML Schema
Input: RDBS Document
Output: XSD Document (XML Schema)
1. Begin
2.   Build Tag <?xml version = "1.0" encoding = "UTF-8"?>
3.   Build Tag <xs:schema xmlns=http://www.w3.org/2001/XMLSchema elementFormDefault="qualified" attributeFormDefault="unqualified">
4.   Select RDBS from the document
5.   Make XML Document.name as RDBS.name
6.   Suppose RDBS has total n table's schemas in it
7.   Loop For i = 1 to n do
8.   Select tablei.name from RDBS
9.   Make tablei.name as elementi.name under XML document
10.   Build Tag <xs:element name="tablei.name">
11.   Suppose tablei.name has total m fields in it
12.   Build Tag <xs:complextype>
13.   Build Tag <xs:sequence>
14.   //for primary key and counting
15.   Build Variable string pArray and int pCount = 0
16.   //for foreign keys and counting
17.   Build Variable string fArray and int fCount = 0
18.   Inner Loop For j = 1 to m do
19.   Select fieldj of tablei
20.   /*under brackets written properties are optional. use if needed*/
21.   Build Tag <xs:element name=" fieldj.name" >
22.   Build Tag <xs:simpleType>
23.   /* xs:xmltype can be either equal to xs:int. xs:string, and xs:dateTime etc.*/
24.   Make fieldj equal to base property mapped to xml type xs:xmltype equally mapped to fieldj.datatype
25.   Build Tag <xs:restriction base="xs:xmltype" >
26.   /* Following conditions are for testing data type constraints*/
27.   Condition IF xs:xmltype is xs:dateTime
28.   Build Tag <xs:minInclusive value="0100-01-01T00:00:00">
29.   Build Tag <xs:maxInclusive value="9999-12-31T23:59:59">
30.   Build Tag <xs:pattern value="\p{Nd}{4}-\p{Nd}{2}-\p{Nd}{2}T\p{Nd}{2}:\p{Nd}{2}:\p{Nd}{2}"/>
31.   Condition Else
32.   /*here temporary variables minLen, maxLen, minValue and maxValue are representative of minimum and maximum value contained for corresponding data type constraint */
33.   /*under brackets written restrictions are optional. use if needed*/
34.   End IF
35.   /* Following conditions are for testing primary key and foreign keys*/
36.   Condition IF fieldj is primary key
37.   /*save value of fieldj.name in pCount iteration of pArray array variable*/
38.   Assign Array Value pArray = fieldj.name
39.   Add one to pCount

```
40.                    Condition Else IF fieldj is foreign key
41.    /*save value of fieldj.tableName. foreign key table name to whom it is primary key. in fCount iteration
of fArray array variable*/
42.                        Assign Array Value fArray = fieldj.tableName
43.                        Add one to fCount
44.                    End IF
45.                End Inner Loop
46.                Inner Loop For k = 1 to fCount-1
47.        Build Tag <xs: element ref= fArray minOccurs = "0" maxOccurs = "unbounded" >
48.                End Inner Loop
49.                Build Tag < xs:sequence>
50.                Build Tag </xs:complextype>
51.                Inner Loop For k = 1 to pCount
52.                    Build Tag <xs:key name=tablei.name +" PrimaryKey"+k>
53.                    Build Tag <xs:selector xpath=","/>
54.                    Build Tag <xs:field xpath= pArray />
55.                    Build Tag </xs:key>
56.                End Inner Loop
57.                Condition IF pCount == 1
58.                    Inner Loop For k = 1 to fCount
59.        Build Tag <xs:keyref name= fArray +"_ForeignKey_"+k refer= tablei.name+"_PrimaryKey_"+1 >
60.                        Build Tag <xs:selector xpath= fArray />
61.                        Build Tag <xs:field xpath= pArray />
62.                        Build Tag <xs:key>
63.                    End Inner Loop
64.                End IF
65.        End Loop
66.        Build Tag < xs:schema>
67. End
```

From the Pursuit of Transformation from RDBS into XML Schema begins by using a feature with termed feature as DB name that becomes father or mother part in the entire XML record. Whereas, sub-elements included in the parent section are all blamed as termed symbolizing as other in XML Schema to every connection at a DB. Subsequently each portion of the connection is an intricate section to possess further straightforward elements instead of areas seen in accompanying terms to DB being altered. Every single field connected component is created such a way that limits relating to discipline's arrangement such as dimension and data type are put within just as limitation tag.

The limit of the algorithm Base execution will likely function as after sequence generated for connections and disciplines in which keeping information in an XML document or it won't have confirmed by W3C evaluation for XML and also XML's syntax and link validity and correspondence.

Algorithm: Transformation from XML Schema to RDFS
Input: XML Document (XML Schema)
Output: RDFS Triples
1. Begin
2.   Select XML Document.name from the document
3.   Build Triple XML Document.name rdfs:Class rdf:resource
4.   * here dot symbol shows property of the document selected*
5.   Suppose XML Document has total n complex elements in it
6.   Loop For i = 1 to n do
7.   Select elementi from XML Document
8.   Selected Tag <xs:elementi name=" elementi.name">
9.   *i-th element of complex type*
10.   Make Triple XML Document.name rdf:Type rdfs:Class
11.   Make Triple elementi.name rdf:Type rdfs:Class
12.   Make Triple elementi.name rdf:subClassOf XML Document.name
13.   Suppose elementi has total m sub elements in its sequence tag
14.   Inner Loop For j = 1 to m do
15.   Select sub-elementj of elementi
16.   Make Triple elementi.name rdf:Property sub-elementj.name
17.   Make Triple sub-elementj.name rdfs:domain elementi.name
18.   Make Triple sub-elementj.name rdfs:range rdfs:Literal
19.   Make Triple sub-elementi.name rdfs:DataType sub-elementj.type
20.   Suppose sub-elementj has q tags under xs:restriction tag
21.   Inner Loop For l = 1 to q do
22.   * tag represents inner tag depending on what element
xs:restriction contains among xs:minInclusive, xs:maxInclusive, xs:minLength and
xs:maxLength*
23.   Switch tagl
24.   Case: xs:minInclusive
25.   Make Triple sub-elementj.name owl:minCardinality
tagl.value
26.   Make Triple sub-elementj.name rdfs:comment
"xs:minInclusive"
27.   Case: xs:maxInclusive
28.   Make Triple sub-elementj.name owl:maxCardinality
tagl.value
29.   Make Triple sub-elementj.name rdfs:comment
"xs:maxInclusive"
30.   Case: xs:minLength
31.   Make Triple sub-elementj.name owl:minCardinality
tagl.value
32.   Make Triple sub-elementj.name rdfs:comment
"xs:minLength"
33.   Case: xs:maxLength
34.   Make Triple sub-elementj.name owl:maxCardinality
tagl.value
35.   Make Triple sub-elementj.name rdfs:comment
"xs:maxLength"
36.   End Inner Loop
37.   Suppose elementi has total p xs:key and xs:keyrefk in it
38.   Inner Loop For k = 1 to p do
39.   Condition IF xs:keyk.
40.   *equivalent to the tag <xs:key name=tablei.name+"
PrimaryKey"+count>*
41.   Make Triple xs:keyk.field.xpath rdfs:isDefinedBy elementi.name
42.   Make Triple xs:keyk.field.xpath rdfs:subPropertyOf elementi.name
43.   Condition Else IF xs:keyrefk
44.   *equivalent to the tag <xs:keyref name= fArray +"_ForeignKey_"+count
refer= tablei.name+"_PrimaryKey_"+1 >*
45.   Make Triple xs:keyrefk.field.xpath rdfs:isDefinedBy
elementi.name
46.   Make Triple xs:keyrefk.field.xpath rdfs:subPropertyOf
xs:keyrefk.selector.xpath
47.   End IF
48.   End Inner Loop
49.   End Loop
50. End

Algorithm: Transformation from XML Schema to RDBS
Input: XML Document (XML Schema)
Output: RDBS Document
1. Begin
2.   Select the root element.name from the document
3.   /* here dot symbol shows the property of the element selected*/
4.   Make the root element.name of DTD equal to RDBS.name
5.   Condition IF (! exists (RDBS.name)) /*check RDB with same name exists or not*/
6.   Build RDB RDBS.name
7.   End IF
8.   Select RDBS RDBS.name
9.   /* here is Relation DB is selected for further operations*/
10.   Suppose XML document has total n elements in it
11.   Loop For i = 1 to n do
12.   Select elementi.name from XML Document
13.   Make tablei.name as elementi.name under RDB
14.   Build Table tablei.name
15.   Select Tag Complextype
16.   /* <xs:complextype> */
17.   Select Tag Sequence
18.   /* <xs:sequence> */
19.   Suppose Sequence has m sub-elements in it
20.   Inner Loop For j = 1 to m do
21.   Select elementj of sequence of elementi
22.   Make fieldj.name= elementj.name
23.   Make fieldj.datatype=elementj.type
24.   Build Field fieldj
25.   End Inner Loop
26.   Condition IF sequence tag ended
27.   Suppose Complex type has k attributes in it
28.   Inner Loop For k = 1 to p
29.   Condition IF attributek.use = "required"
30.   Build Field fieldm+k.name= attributek.name fieldm+k.datatype= attributek.type
31.   Make Primary Key fieldm+k
32.   Condition Else
33.   Build Field fieldm+k.name= attributek.name fieldm+k.datatype= attributek.type
34.   Make Foreign Key fieldm+k
35.   End IF
36.   End Inner Loop
37.   End IF
38.   End Loop
39. End

3.6 Mapping of XML Tags

Three calculations are all Designed to Cover information interpretation and an annotation about the grounds of grading mechanism invented in the mathematical division.

Algorithm 1 : TranslateTag( ) Translates corresponding tag into RDF tag

---
Input : *number of items* (*n*); *value recorded* ; *type of each item* (*type*); *recoded instant at time t*
Output : *list of annotated* (⟨*tags*⟩) *XML element*
1. *Collect data generated* **from** *the sensor S*
2.**for** *decision iterator i* := 1 **to** *n* **do**
3.**if** $P^r\left(t', x_c^t\right) \leq 1$ *according* **to** *Formula* (3)
4. *extract each row* **and** *tag it as an element*
5. *close the each corresponding tag*
6. *List L* := *add element*
7.**end if**
8.**end for**
9.**return** *list L*

Algorithm 1 is accepting worth Made by detectors and conducting it throughout action comprised by representatives Based on Eq. (3) the formulation to determine its fitness centre to be interpreted into a label. Subsequently, every label centred schema will be Together having its value is both produced and as stated by the W3C specifications for XML tags, so each label is shut so in Announcement 5 and 4. All created tags have been additionally saved in a listing to be Came back into the calling role for worried TranslateTag() Algorithm.

Algorithm 2 : *GenerateTriple( ) Generation of corresponding list of triples for given XML tag*

Input : *number of tags* (n)*; type of each tag* $(type)$
Output : *list of annotated* $(\langle tags \rangle)$ *XML / RDF*
1. *Expand each tag*
2.**for** *decision iterator i :=* 1 **to** *n* **do**
   // number of tags contained within an element
3.**if** *tag*[*i*].*isElement( )* = 1
   // isElement( ) returns 1 *when current tag is element*
4. *extract each tag* **and** *annotate it as triple*
5. *generate unique id* **for** *new resource*
6. *List T := add triples*
7.**end if**
8.**end for**
9.**return** *list T*

Algorithm 2 further transforms XML tags right into RDF triples. Record 3 is evaluation built to enter being the whole label by arriving inch under exactly the procedure named is an element (). Each Re-Source generated in this conversion procedure new identification is presented about the grounds of formerly non- presence. All produced triples are farther saved in a list to be returned into the calling role to worried GenerateTriple().

Algorithm 3 : *Transformation* from *Sensor Data into Annotated RDF Format*

Input : *Data File* **to** *annotate, type of each data item* $(type)$
Output : *annotated* $(\langle tags \rangle)$ *item into triple reduced* **from** *original*
1. *Collect data generated* **from** *the sensor S*
2. *Repeat until EOF // End of File* (EOF)
3. *annotated List L := GenerateTriple(TranslateTag( ))*
   // according **to** *Algo* 1 **and** 2
4. *End Loop*

Algorithm 3 is currently using the algorithms 1 and 2 completed for an upgraded set of triples in announcement 3. The total input signal is read statement two beneath a loop keeping from A-list listing L. Now to Figure out the timing Sophistication of these calculations at this conversation. Let us think about, and Tj symbolize time sophistication for algorithm j against announcement i will be symbolized since Ti leading to the kind of upper and lower jump from using Θ (theta) signal where j=1,2,3 and $1 \le i \le 9$.

Following is the time complexity T1(n) generated by Algorithm 1:

T1(n)= T1+T2+T3+...+T9

T1(n)=1+n (1+1+1+1+1+1+1)

T1(n)= 1+7n= Θ(n)

Following is the time complexity T2(n) generated by Algorithm 2:

T2(n)= T1+T2+T3+...+T9

T2(n)=1+n (1+1+1+1+1+1+1)

T2(n)=1+7n= Θ(n)

Following is the time complexity T3(n) generated by Algorithm 3:

T3(n)= T1+T2+T3+T4

T3(n)=1+n+n(n(n)) +1

T3(n)=1+n+n3+1= Θ(n3)

Finally, the resultant time complexity T(n) for proposed model implementation through algorithms is:

T(n)=T1(n)+T2(n)+T3(n)= Θ(n3)

Data Transformation Algorithms

Mathematical Modeling

The best information in Bigdata looks in 4 formats Online Video, Audio, Textual, and Graphics. Table 3 signifies the language Employed in mathematical modelling.

Table 3: Definitions of terms used in mathematical modelling

Notation	Description
V	A set of all video contents
W	A set of all words
I	A set of all images
A	A set of all sound data
T	XML set of interlinked data using tags
t	Tag representing element for XML
k	Total number of tags having opened and closing
n	Total number of tags to represent an information
S	Source for RDF triple
R	Resource for RDF triple
P	The predicate for RDF triple

Now let us first Establish the reflective kind of XML information to get a certain slice of details

$$X = \frac{\ln(t)}{\ln(2)} + t$$

$$t = e^{-\text{LambertW}\left(\ln(2)\, e^{X\ln(2)}\right) + X\ln(2)}$$

$$\therefore (t) \in T$$

Where t belongs to the family of a set of XML; now let's take a function X_t

$$X_t = \left(\frac{k\,\ln(k)}{\ln(2)} + n - k \right) t \tag{1}$$

$$\because k, n \in \mathbb{N}$$

This $k\,\log_2(k)$ signifies all labels together with closing and opening tags, whereas $(n - k)$ are staying individual labels in XML underneath certain advice representation. Eq. (1) X_t May Offer a Comprehensive pair of tags to Represent advice

If $a = k\,\log_2(k) + (n - k)$ then

$$a = \frac{k\,\ln(k)}{\ln(2)} + n - k \tag{2}$$

By putting the value of Eq. (2) in Eq. (1)

$$X_t = a\,t \tag{3}$$

For constant increase of data on time basis Eq. (3) becomes

$$X_t = a\,t + 2a\,t + 3a\,t + 4a\,t + \ldots + m a\,t$$

$$X_t = \frac{1}{2}\, m(m-1)\,\lambda\, a\, t \tag{4}$$

If change is constant, then constant factor lambda lies between

$$0 < \lambda \le 1 \tag{5}$$

Where $m \in \mathbb{N}$ and m is a maximum change which can occur in an instance

$$X_t = \begin{vmatrix} a\,t & \lambda > 0 \\ \dfrac{m(m-1)}{2}\,\lambda\, a\, t & \lambda \le 1 \end{vmatrix} \tag{6}$$

Substantial information when Translated into XML sort comprise worth and schema for several sorts of contents that call for to take good care of. Eq. (6) exhibits the need for the shift variable in our instance lambda that remains non-effective if the nearest zero. For your collection of Online Video/tags may be symbolized at the sort of t_v for XML purpose X_{tv} and likewise, pair of Audio A tags may be reflected at the Shape of/to XML Feature X_{ta}, collection of Phrase tags could be symbolized at the kind of/to XML purpose X_{tw} and ultimately pair of Graphics tags may be symbolized at the Shape of/for XML purpose X_{ti}

$$X_{tv} = \begin{vmatrix} a\,t & \lambda > 0 \\ \dfrac{m(m-1)}{2}\,\lambda\, a\, t_v & \lambda \le 1 \end{vmatrix}$$

$$X_{ta} = \begin{vmatrix} a\,t & \lambda > 0 \\ \dfrac{m(m-1)}{2}\,\lambda\, a\, t_a & \lambda \le 1 \end{vmatrix}$$

$$X_{tw} = \begin{cases} a\,t & \lambda > 0 \\ \dfrac{m(m-1)}{2}\,\lambda\,a\,t_{t_w} & \lambda \le 1 \end{cases}$$

$$X_{ti} = \begin{cases} a\,t & \lambda > 0 \\ \dfrac{m(m-1)}{2}\,\lambda\,a\,t_{t_i} & \lambda \le 1 \end{cases}$$

$$X_{bigdata} = X_{tv} + X_{ta} + X_{tw} + X_{t_i} \qquad (7)$$

Eq. (7) May Be your Basic sort of XML information interpreted for information revealed in just about any sort of In-Coming data contents that were big. We could even state that:

$$(X_{tv}) \approx (X_{ta} + X_{tw} + X_{ti}) \qquad (8)$$

Eq. (8) can simply Be authentic if forthcoming out of an identical origin and at this scenario Eq. (7) will seem like

$$X_{bigdata} = X_{tv} + X_{tv}$$

$$X_{bigdata} = 2\,X_{tv}$$

Let T is a set of all tag sets $\{T_1, T_2, T_3, T_4, \cdots, T_n\}$ where each element of T is a set as $\subseteq T$

In RDF each T_i tag set is transformed into multiple linked triples of (S, P, O) set R_i

$$R_i = \{(S_1, P_1, O_1), (S_2, P_2, O_2), (S_3, P_3, O_3), \cdots, (S_k, P_k, O_k)\} \qquad (9)$$

Where k is the possible triple value of the corresponding/tag set? The RDF complete set be

$$R = \{R_1, R_2, R_3, R_4, \cdots, R_m\} \; \because m \in \mathbb{N}$$

Here m is the real number representing a maximum set produced for a specific XML data. According to Eq. (5) and Eq. (9) it can be said

$$R_T = R + \lambda R' \qquad (10)$$

In Eq. (10) λ is the same as defined in Eq. (4) same change factor and R' is new RDF triples added to old set R at the instance T

The boost from the Value of λ seems as a result of battle, duplications, fast Rising linkage, and crashes in information generated the kind of RDF. It is Be decreased by diminishing the level of sophistication of transformation in the Degree of information representation of data that is big. There's a requirement of restraining variable, which may connect data favorably during that time that it's already been generated. This controller can Be attained on the verge of XML production. Every single datum may likewise use Classification from meta-data to find out connected data resources and intention.

3.6.1 Mapping Functions

Agents Will Probably Likely Be Concentrating on the time-oriented classification of Information from Fitting mechanics of purchasing of each instantaneous phenomenon. Pairing mechanism one of the brokers is awarded in respect one follows:

A Matching Representations between $m \in$ *XML profiles* at Eq. (1) and $c \in$ *Current Captures* at Eq. (2), at time $t_n \in$ *Time*, as X_m and X_c^m, forming sequence $\left(x_c^{t_1}, x_c^{t_2}, x_c^{t_3}, \ldots \right)$ with $t_1 \leq t_2 \leq \cdots \leq t_n$, where:

For everyone i,

$$x_c^i [j] \in \left[\min_j^c, \max_j^c \right] \tag{1}$$

$$x_m [j] \in \left[\min_j^m, \max_j^m \right] \tag{2}$$

with $i = 1, 2, 3, \cdots$

Definition 2 (Pattern Recognition)

Given a resource r (could be any category of data) and its scoring functions S^r, r's pattern recognition at time t' of individual's match value x^t for a time $t < t'$, is defined as:

$$P^r \left(t', x_c^t \right) = \begin{cases} reject & \text{if } t' > t^r \text{ or } S\left(x^{t'} \right) < 1 \\ add\ one & \text{if } S\left(x_c^{t'} \right) \approx S^r\left(x_m^t \right) \\ x^t & otherwise \end{cases} \tag{3}$$

A Case Study: Transforming a DB into RDF and back into DB, as shown in Figure 10, and the graphical representation of transforming a DB into RDF and back into DB, as shown in Figure 11.

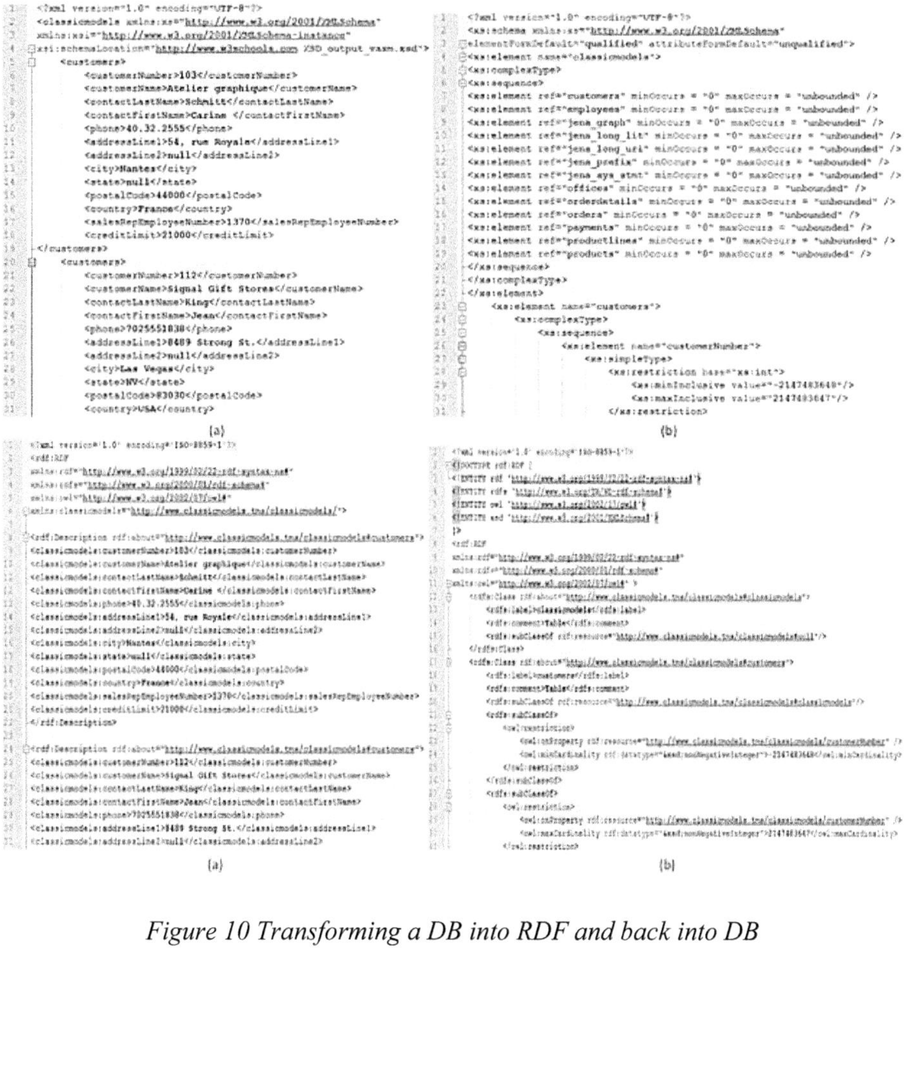

Figure 10 Transforming a DB into RDF and back into DB

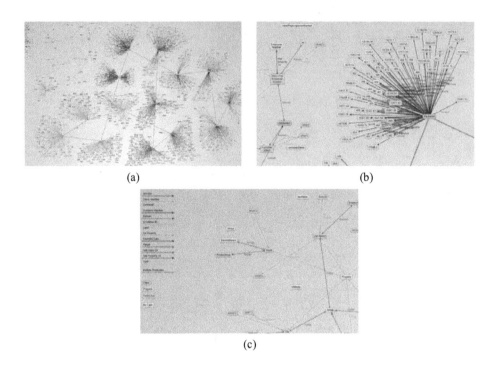

(a)　　　　　　　　　　　　　　(b)

(c)

Figure 11 The graphical representation of transforming a DB into RDF and back into DB

Primary key-based triple extraction, as shown in Figure 12, and foreign keys and composite keys based triple extraction, as shown in Figure 13.

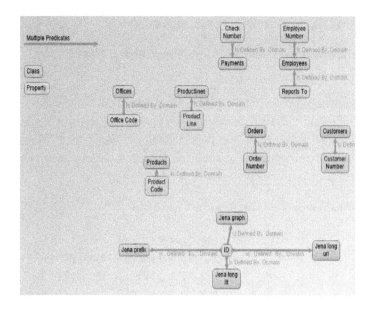

Figure 12 Primary Key based Triple Extraction

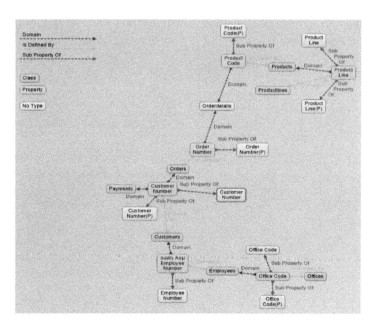

Figure 13 Foreign Keys and Composite Keys based Triple Extraction

4 IMPLEMENTING PROPOSED RESEARCH

4.1 Transformation of English Lexicon Tags into RDB Tuples

The first stage of transformation has been launched together with consumer input. That is, in fact, a series. When technique gets an input signal, this really can be converted to tags/Synsets thought to be the first conversion endeavor. Meanwhile, the agents have been triggered (JADE) to obtain their individual label/lexicon, then its center accountability of representatives to conserve those lexicons into their various desk of database termed as "mydb".

4.2 Transformation of Simple Text into Lexicons

An individual can enter a series at the System, which will be Moved to WordNet. WordNet will likewise talk about the written text using Stanford parser. Stanford parser would emphasize the obtained series to parts. Subsequently, against just about every token, its parts of speech (POS) sort is returned, which is the token consists of a noun, noun, adverb or adjective sort POS (Malik et al., 2020). Stanford parser is taught by code to unite just about every token along with its particular POS to an Array List, and right after the conclusion of the action, this life-sized set is plotted as it pertains to this subpar action to execute the additional activity. A stream of tasks conducted is displayed in Figure 14.

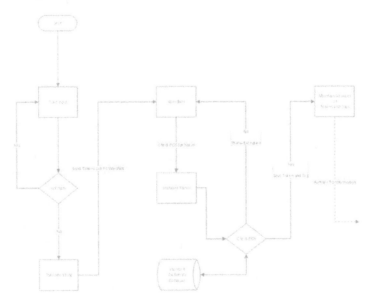

Figure 14: Transformation of Text into Tags/Synsets

50

Guidelines to tokenize the input then transform the series to parts and are composed in Java. Afterwards, as a result of Java guidelines, the Tokenized series is inputted to WordNet to get additional processing, which could move tokenized series to Stanford Parser. A photo of employed code Is Offered under, as shown in Figure 15.

```
28      public static ArrayList parseString(String sent) throws IOException, Exception
29  □ {
30
31
32          String grammar = "edu/stanford/nlp/models/lexparser/englishPCFG.ser.gz";
33          String[] options = { "-maxLength", "500", "-retainTmpSubcategories" };
34          LexicalizedParser lp = LexicalizedParser.loadModel(grammar, options);
35          TreebankLanguagePack tlp = lp.getOp().langpack();
36          GrammaticalStructureFactory gsf = tlp.grammaticalStructureFactory();
37
38          Iterable<List<? extends HasWord>> sentences;
39
40          Tokenizer<? extends HasWord> toke =
41          tlp.getTokenizerFactory().getTokenizer(new StringReader(sent));
42          List<? extends HasWord> sentence2 = toke.tokenize();
43
44          List<List<? extends HasWord>> tmp =
            new ArrayList<List<? extends HasWord>>();
46          tmp.add(sentence2);
47          sentences = tmp;
48
49          Tree parse = lp.parse(sent);
50
51          taggedString = parse.taggedYield();
52
53          return taggedString;
54  └ }
```

Figure 15: Java Code to get tags for tokens and then store into Array List variable tagged String

Even Though libraries contained for attracting from the operation of both Stanford Parser and WordNet have been offered in Figure 16.

```
 2
 3 ⊟  import java.io.IOException;
 4 │  import java.io.StringReader;
 5 │  import java.util.*;
 6 │
 Q⃥ │  import edu.stanford.nlp.ling.CoreLabel;
 8 │  import edu.stanford.nlp.ling.HasWord;
 Q⃥ │  import edu.stanford.nlp.ling.Label;
 Q⃥ │  import edu.stanford.nlp.ling.TaggedWord;
 Q⃥ │  import edu.stanford.nlp.ling.Word;
 Q⃥ │  import edu.stanford.nlp.process.*;
 Q⃥ │  import edu.stanford.nlp.parser.lexparser.*;
 Q⃥ │  import edu.stanford.nlp.process.DocumentPreprocessor;
15 │  import edu.stanford.nlp.process.Tokenizer;
16 │  import edu.stanford.nlp.trees.*;
17 └  import edu.stanford.nlp.parser.lexparser.LexicalizedParser;
18
```

Figure 16: Packages imported for using WordNet and Stanford Parser
Functionalities

4.3   Creating and managing JADE Agents

Once labels have been coming back in Array List, representatives have been manufactured by utilizing Jade to look at on the labels by you and also obtain advice about label and classifieds to save from relational database to get their individual POS (part of Speech) facts. There are Essential, five brokers are Made, and their Titles are determined by based on operation/faculties they've. Agents generated are everywhere also, Agent_Verb, Agent_Noun, Agent_Adjective, Agent_MicsPOS, and Agent_Adverb.

Agent_Noun oversees Find noun kind of label and its Ignore, initiate relationship series with a database, which is"mydb" established in MySQL. The information that will be stored within relational DB maybe your centre accountability of Noun_Agent; in the event, the kind of label acquired is of noun variety (Farhan et al.).

The same pair of duties would be all for verb, adverb, adjective, and mic spots sort representatives to get their label and nominal information and certainly will save. Once preserving that advice, brokers are shifted their condition out of busy to sleep before the next blossom of the same sort is acquired to execute the same activity differently. Agents generated originally Have Been in the suspended manner, and it's already been observable out of Jade distant Agent administration GUI display taken provided beneath as found as shown in Figure 17.

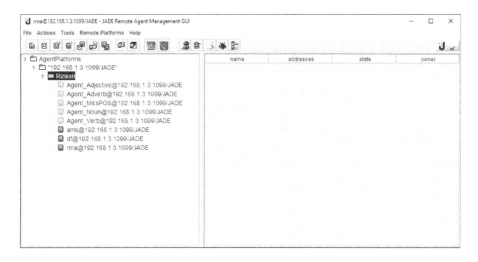

Figure 17: Agents creation and suspended state showed

As exhibited in the figure, all brokers are still in a suspended manner. Initially, every time a specific label is obtained, the concerned broker is resumed and made to execute its actions and again go in suspension condition. In Figure 18, a busy representative of sort Agent_Adverb is proven in GUI, which is currently active in keeping information from the database.

Figure 18: Agent_Adverb inactive state

4.4 Storing information in DB by JADE Agents

By representative, subsequently, the relationship is created between a broker and MySQL"mydb" database, and the record has been added into the database. Subsequently, the representative would shut the database connection session then switched into its busy condition back into a frozen state. The representatives are still in conversation with all relational databases. Relational Database Entity terms version will be introduced to Get a Chicken eye evaluation of mydb database rational layout and posing since exhibited in Figure 19.

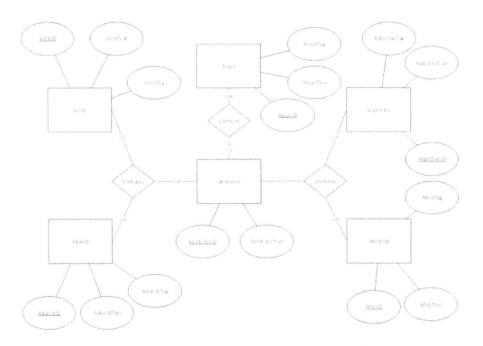

Figure 19: ER diagram of mydb Database

You will find just six things included in every other in ERD of all mydb. However, few situations, each text contains POS that doesn't drop in almost any one of big classification; to deal with this occurrence MicsPOS thing is styled. And sentence thing can be found to deal with all sorts of paragraphs/strings/text which can be handed to WordNet to get tokenizing/accessing tags. You do a lot of connection exist amongst Sentence and each of the additional five things. Quantity of features will be the same for stuff apart from the sentencing entity. Features include one feature that's utilized to take care of ID of this POS, and the next feature is tackling text/lexicon and label WordNet// Stanford Parser attracts that. At the same time, the keyword thing contains just two features, which can be ID along with the text. When shredding methods have been Utilized to alter the ER diagram into a relational schema, the resulting schema got for the mydb database has been given in Figure 20.

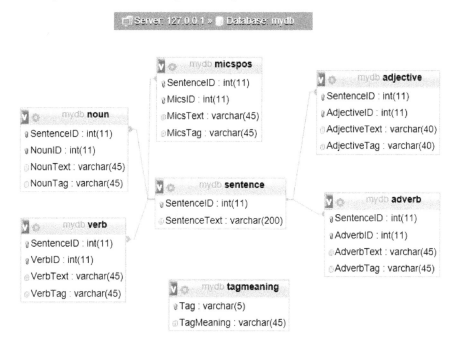

Figure 20: Relational Schema obtained for mydb after transforming its ERD

Few developments in the schema are talked about the following. As your feature is inserted in five tables, tackling POS that's Sentence ID. It is because of relational mapping of ER, as Sentence table has connections of you to a lot of together with each table; therefore a foreign key will be inserted in a single table that's also utilized as a part of the primary key with the ID of the table to make the composite key as shown in Table 4. Present-day, a brand-new code has been mentioned in Table 5, which can exhibit generation of brokers, database management, and handling of all brokers.

Table 4 the primary key with the ID of the table to make composite key.

1 - sql = "Select Max(NounID) as Max from Noun where sentenceID =" + maxVal;

2 - ResultSet rs1 = stmt.executeQuery(sql);

3 - rs1.next();

4 - maxNoun = rs1.getInt("Max")+1;

5 - rs1.close();

Table 5: Pseudocode for Agent creation and management

1 – Launch JADE Agent Platform

2 – Create 5 agents with name Agent_Noun, Agent_Verb, Agent_Adverb, Agent_Adjective and Agent_MicsPOS

3 – Set states of agents as Suspended

4 – Get tagged String

5 – Loop: until tagged String is not empty

    5.1 – Get tag

    5.2a – If tag contains NN then Agent_Noun state is set as active

    5.2b – else if tag contains VB then Agent_Verb state is set as active

    5.2c – else if tag contains JJ then Agent_Adjective state is set as active

    5.2d – else if tag contains RB then Agent_Adverb state is set as active

    5.2e – else then Agent_MicsPOS state is set as active

6 – Call for DB-Function

7 – Suspend State set for activated agent

8 – End Loop   // Starting from 5

In the ending of the chapter, even a diagram symbolizing whole Procedure for the conversion is furnished below is an extension of Figure 21.

Figure 21: complete flow diagram of Transformation from text to Relational DB

4.5 Transformation of RDB Tuples into XML and XSD

Secondly, the transformation of thesis research would be to Change relational D B tuples to eXtensible Markup Language (XML) schema and document. Extension of all XML schema document is *.XML and *.XSD to get the XML file. In sooner stage, an Easy text/lexicon is changed To Synsets or even Tags with the assistance of Java representatives (JADE), the tags have been stored within the relational database in their various table. You will find just two sub Jobs which are done within this Transformation, which are scanning database schema, then transform it to XML schema as well as at the next period, relational DB will be examined to alter values on it into an XML file. Both major transformations are clarified in segments provided below.

4.6 Transformation of Relational DB Schema into XML Schema

4.6.1 Reading Relational DB Schema

At the measure, to Start with, we import SQL libraries to utilize SQL coffee qualities to browse/publish to MySQL Database. An association series is created to get a"mydb" database characterized in MySQL. By way of this relationship series, the relationship having a database has been created. Afterwards, the question is implemented to see

57

meta-data of database which have titles of most tables set in of "mydb" relational database. The table list is saved within just collection listing for prospective usage. Once afterwards, a loop has been implemented which could implement before we browse titles of most tables within it. Through this loop, we're becoming some simple information on the topic of the table, which has maximum and minimum happenings in a table together side advice of essential elements which have information regarding primary keywords/mix secret of this table and important foreign limitations. The information can be plotted to a list of series variety.

While studying fundamental advice about the table, we present you with More loop in it to browse column advice about the table. Column advice includes the title of the pillar. Additional read advice is minimal and optimum values of this column together side data variety. The information will be stored in ArrayList utilized early in the day to save information. Thus, after implementing this loop, finally, we're capable of getting all advice about our specified tables, their columns together side limitations employed on them. An algorithm/pseudo code is displayed previously in, which comprises advice of most described ways, as shown in Table 6.

Table 6: Pseudocode for reading database and column information (Meta Data)

1 – Establish connection to database with help of connection string

2- Information regarding names of tables is being extracted

3 – Stored Table Names in database "mydb" in ArrayList

4 – Loop: until read names of all tables one by one

    4.1 – Read Minimum occurrences allowed in table

    4.2 – Read Maximum occurrences allowed in table

    4.3 – Get Primary Key information

    4.4 – Get Foreign Key information

    4.5 – Loop: until read all column information

        4.5.1 – Get column Name

        4.5.2 – Get minimum value of column

        4.5.3 – Get maximum column value

        4.5.4 – Extract information regarding data type of column

    4.6 – End Inner Loop

    4.7 – Store all read information along with table name in Array List

5 – End Outer Loop

6 - End

4.6.2 Reading ArrayList and Writing XSD File

This measure, initially, we present a couple of header tags of XML Containing advice regarding XML versioning and schema communicating advice and course (if any). Then, and element1 style label is launched featuring identify of the database, which is "mydb." A complicated type label is followed closely by a part label containing advice of most tables included in disc together with advice regarding maximum and minimum occurrences of tuples, particularly table. All these table titles ought to take an arrangement and cited previously in XSD record as arrangement style element2. Minimum happenings are characterized as in many instances if perhaps not specifically place throughout the production of the desk. While default, maximum happenings are cited as unbound (unmentioned/virtually infinite). Every label is suitably closed the moment it begins. Once final of intricate sort element3, the procedure for writing advice about each table has been initiated from the onset of part type label, it could comprise all advice regarding desk, which comprises, identify of columns, advice regarding keys (primary and foreign), limitations, information kind of column, minute, and maximum worth of the column. The information of the table's column is defined as a complex type, while constraints information is defined as simple type elements4.

- Element is everything that contains all information from start to end of the tag.
- The values must be in sequence.
- Type of element that contains other elements within it
- A simple type element is an element containing values of defined attributes.

These specified labels/components and browse data Are composed in still another ArrayList that by the finish is known to Java code to compose a document which kind is thought as XSD. A standard algorithm that's adopted to do XSD composing endeavour is offered. Now, code for writing XSD file by using ArrayList in java is provided below in Table 7.

Table 7: Pseudocode for writing XML schema in ArrayList

1 – Write XML version and start schema tags

2 – Define database name tag as element type

3 – Start complex type tag along with sequence tag

3 – Loop: until all table name are read

    3.1 – Write table name as element reference

    3.2 – Write minimum and maximum occurrences

4 – End Loop

5 – End sequence tag and then complex type tag

6 – Loop: until all table names are read

    6.1 – Start element type tag with value of table name

    6.2 – Start Complex type tag and then sequence tag

    6.3 – Loop: until all columns of table are read

        6.3.1 – Start element type tag with name as table name then start sequence tag

        6.3.2 – Start element tag with value of attribute name

        6.3.3 – Start simple type element and then restriction tag along with data type

        6.3.4 – Mention minimum and maximum value of particular column

        6.3.5 – End restriction tag and then simple tag

        6.3.6 – End element tag that was started for column

    6.4 – End sequence tag and then complex type tag

    6.5 – End Loop   // Reading column Loop

    6.6 – Start key tag containing keys information

4.6.3 Data flow diagram of Transformation

Transformation of DB to XML schema entails two important Steps which are reading through relational database schema and also metadata reading and moment is currently writing of XSD document around the grounds of both Advice study from database which has been talked about in more detail. This Entire Procedure Is pictorially exhibited using a flow graph structure, as shown in Figure 22 and Table 8.

Table 8: Code for writing XML schema file in Java using ArrayList

```
String fileName = "XSD_output_"+fName+".xsd";

FileWriter fileWriter = new FileWriter(fileName);

BufferedWriter bufferedWriter = new BufferedWriter(fileWriter);

for(int i=0; i< container.size(); i++)

{        // Container is ArrayList Object containing all information described in table 2a and 2b

        bufferedWriter.write((String)container.get(i));

}

bufferedWriter.close();
```

Figure 22: Flow diagram of Transformation of DB Schema into XML Schema

4.7   Transformation of Relational DB tuples into XML

Now next stage of conversion would always be to see information/tuples/worth out of database tables and compose it from XML document based on World Wide Web Consortium (W3C) specified regulations. This conversion additionally comprises two subpar actions that are already reading out of write and database information in ArrayList appropriately. And second, transform this composed ArrayList from an XML file.

4.7.1 Reading Relational DB tuples

At the measure, to begin with, we import SQL libraries to utilize SQL coffee characteristics to browse/publish to MySQL Database. An association series is created to get "mydb" database characterized as shown in Table 9.

Table 9: Pseudocode for reading database Record Set and Schema

1 – Establish connection to database with help of connection string

2- Information regarding names of tables is being extracted

3 – Stored Table Names in database "mydb" in ArrayList

4 – Loop: until read names of all tables one by one

    4.1 – Loop: until read all column information

        4.1.1 – Read column Name

        4.1.2 – Extract information regarding data type of column

    4.2 – End Loop   // Read column name and type

    4.3 – Get Record Set of table

    4.4 – Loop: Until Record Set of table returns NULL

        4.4.1 - Store record in ArrayList

        4.4.2 – Type cast record values into string if not in string type

    4.5 – End Loop   // Reading Record Set

5 – Store all read information along with table name in Array List

5 – End Outer Loop

6 - End

MySQL. By way of this relationship series, the relationship having a database has been created. Afterwards, the question is implemented to see meta-data of database which have titles of most tables set in of "mydb" relational database. The table list is saved within just collection listing for prospective usage, right after reading fundamental advice of names. A loop has been launched that select titles of the desk by you by the checklist. A question is implemented to bring a listing collection of desks (all of the tuples within this table) and some simple advice about pillar titles along with their information kind. We present yet another fold over it to learn attracted advice of pillar of the table. When the price is of integer form, then it's kindly caked to save since series. All this information will be stored in ArrayList for prospective users to compose the XML file. The information can be plotted to a list of series variety. (An integral coffee data sort ArrayList can be utilized to save that information.) Thus, after implementing this loop, finally, we're capable of getting all advice of tuples of tables that are defined. An algorithm/pseudo code is displayed previously in desk 6-4, which comprises advice of most described ways.

4.8   Writing XML File

At the next step, we'd parse the data of File Establish first period of scanning database. Much like element 6.1.2, ArrayList information arrangement can be utilized, begin with, save all of the XML file layouts in it, and then lets Java file reader app to compose XML file.

In the beginning, procedure, launching headers will be contained that Contains information about XML variation. Secondly, meta tags are schema advice labels, commence with all titles of the database, which is "mydb" in our instance. This label also has namespace advice to demonstrate that attributes and elements will be arriving out of the foundation recorded adjoining to XS prefix. A regional XML schema can be known in this label to assist while supporting the XML record in opposition to XSD. The location of all XSD documents is cited because of re-Source at XSI prefix. Introductory tags for XML have been ended for this specific.

Next-to opening XML tags, information features, and worth Are all styled in XML record. ArrayList, which comprises Record Place advice of tables, is pulled and parsed to find table columns and data against just about every pillar. As stated in portion, 6.2.1, information aside from series is type throw to series.

Contain tags, so could begin out of table title afterwards one album Will be examining. Each pillar name will be taken care of as feature which could start as label subsequently appraise contrary to the pillar and column name label is shut. Then the second column is launched as a tag, which will replicate the method until a tuple is prepared in XML mode in ArrayList.

The same procedure can replicate itself to the entire table after which for All tables. The tables comprising no worth in it's not going to demonstrate any label in XML document writeup because their album collection is already empty. Following finishing the entire procedure, the XML record will shut with the name of the database, which has been started in sooner measure.

XML record pattern is composed in ArrayList, which can pass to file author Java code exactly the like clarified in desk 6-3 but together with the reversal of record name along with its stored expansion as.XML. Sample XML photographs generated from a clarified course of action are connected in the Appendix, determine A-2-1, and determine A-2-2. Procedure for keeping XML routine and composing as XML record is displayed from the pseudocodes as shown in Table 10 and Table 11.

Table 10: Pseudocode for writing XML file blueprint in ArrayList

1 – Write XML version tag

2 – Write XML schema tag start with database name

    2.1 – XML namespace prefix is mentioned with xmlns: XS prefix

    2.2 – XML Schema reference as schema location is also mentioned with XSI prefix

3 – Loop: until read names of all tables

    3.1 – Loop: until read all tuples within table

    3.2 – Mention table name as start tag

    3.3 – Loop: until one tuple record is finished

        3.3.1 – Start attribute name tag

        3.3.2 – Write attribute value

        3.3.3 – End attribute name tag

    3.4 – End Loop   // Started from 3.3

    3.5 – Close table name tag

    3.6 – End Loop   // Started from 3.1

4 – End Loop   //Started from 3

5 – Write closing tag of schema as table name

6 - End

Table 11: Writing XML file from ArrayList using Java file writer

```
String fileName = "XSD_output_"+fName+".xml";
FileWriter fileWriter = new FileWriter(fileName);
BufferedWriter bufferedWriter = new BufferedWriter(fileWriter);
for(int i=0; i< container.size(); i++)
{       // Container is ArrayList Object containing all information described in table 2a and 2b
        bufferedWriter.write((String)container.get(i));
}
bufferedWriter.close();
```

4.8.1 Data Flow diagram of Transformation (DB to XML)

Transformation of DB to XML entails two Big Measures which Are studying relational database tuples from the shape of listing collections which are from tables (one particular album collection for a single desk) and next will be writing about XML document around the grounds of advice readout of database which has been shared in more detail from preceding. The whole Procedure Is pictorially exhibited using a flow graph diagram, as shown in Figure 23.

Figure 23: Transformation process flow chart from DB tuples to XML

4.9 Transformation of XSD and XML into RDF Schema and RDF

A third and final but significant stage of transformation of Thesis study would be to alter XSD and XML to source Description Framework (RDF) schema and RDF file. Extension of both RDF schema and RDF document is like. *RDF. In the 2nd stage of transformation, either synsets and Tags saved in Relational database in their various desk have been changed into XML and XSD. You will find just two sub Jobs which are done within this Transformation, which are scanning XML schema to alter at equal RDF Schema as well as in the next period; XML document has been switched into RDF document that's equivalent Into XML document and follows RDF schema. Both significant transformations Are clarified in segments given below.

4.9.1 Transformation of XML Schema (XSD) into RDF Schema

4.9.1.1 Reading XML Schema

At the measure, we emphasize XSD Around the Grounds of both segregations of all Database information composed in it. To start with, we divide XML versioning advice supplied in the XSD record. Secondly, the advice label is bl off since it clarifies XML W3C principles for XSD. Secondly, advice about the consideration is a part label which could comprise advice of the parent part, and in our instance, it's a database about which cornerstone XSD is made. Collars of pubs element labels are additionally listed for understood about tables we all consume, and those were in an arrangement. The next tag is part label after DB advice, which possesses table information. We also recorded information of columns of the database together side their datatypes, minimum and maximum happenings. The advice of secrets (foreign and primary keys) has been extracted from XSD. The technique was repeated before we've required facts of each of the tables as well as their columns together side secrets along with cardinalities facts.

All this information was recorded in different variables and lists that were used later for writing RDF schema. While studying advice about XSD, we present three more loops. Two interior loops have been all used. It's employed for reading through columns and limitations of the desk, while moment can be utilized to figure keys out. Thus, after implementing this loop, finally, we're capable of getting all advice about our specified aspects, their specified attributes together side limitations employed on them. An algorithm/pseudo code is displayed previously in Table 12, which comprises advice of most described ways.

Table 12: Pseudocode for reading XML Schema

1 – Get XML version information

2 – Get parent element information declared in XSD

    2.1 – Read all tags within complex type tag that containing list of tables in sequence

    2.2 – Store all tags / table names in list

3 – Loop: until all tables are read

    3.1 – Find element tag with name equals to name of table in the list

    3.2 – Loop: until elements tags exist within complex type tag

        3.2.1 – Store element as column of table

        3.2.2 – Read restrictions tag to get info of base that is column's data type

        3.2.3 – Read min inclusive tag along with value

        3.2.4 – Read max inclusive tag along with value

    3.3 – End Loop   // Starting from 3.2

    3.4 – Read key tag with key name

    3.5 – Loop: until key tag is closed

        3.5.1 - Read field tag with XPath

    3.6 – End Loop   // Starting from 3.5

4 – End Loop   // Starting from 3

5 - End

4.9.2 Reading ArrayList and Writing RDF Schema File

In this measure, in the beginning, we present a handful of header tags. The First Introduced label consists of an XML variant advice label since it had been cited previously in the XSD file. Then the DOCTYPE remark label is launched; it has an optional label that exhibits the information regarding RDF. It isn't gathered/confirmed throughout parsing. Then the RDF label is launched together side schema namespace using RDF, RDF's, and owl prefixes. All these prefixes are defining the origin of regulations, which can be followed closely through getting ready RDF schema doc. OWL is short to get ontology language. OWL languages have been distinguished by formal semantics language. Thus, the OWL prefix is likewise given in RDF schema to reflect W3C principles. After launching tags, then a course tag of RDF is made, which Comprises reference ID as a piece of the database that's pulled from the XML part tag while looking at the XSD file. This label is represented by tags termed as a tag, opinions, and subpar type of labels.

Still, another type label is launched that's mention ID as Table Name accompanied with exact labels as clarified previously. Before the final category label, a fresh label is started to compose columns/columns of the desk. For composing features, the sub-par labels can be used to define limitations on a feature just like minimal cardinality together side data sort of feature and minimal value it has then for optimum cardinality together with the same features shared previously. Thus, for each feature, just two limitation tags have been all opened. A closing label such as class has already been introduced. From then on, possessions for every single feature is written and registered. Property label comprises sub-par zero tags of advice labels comprising advice including characterized by sub land of, tag, remark, assortment, and domain names.

This process is repeated until, eventually, most of the aspects of tables have been forged with tags in ArrayList, which will be further moved to document author Java code to compose the RDF Schema file. A sample RDF Schema picture generated from the clarified procedure is connected in Appendix a 3, Determine A-3-1, and Determine A-3-2. A standard algorithm that's adopted to execute RDF Schema composing endeavour is offered in Table 13.

Table 13: Writing RDF Schema into ArrayList

1 – Write XML version tag
2 – Write DOCTYPE tag
3 – Start RDF tag
3.1 – Write RDF namespace

3.2 – Write RDFS namespace

3.3 – Write OWL namespace

4 – Start class tag with reference ID as database name

4.1 – Write label tag

4.2 – Write comment tag

4.3 – Write sub class of tag

5 – Loop: until all attributes of element tag is read

5.1 – Start Class tag with reference ID as table name

5.2 – Write label tag

5.3 – Write comment tag

5.4 – sub class of tag

5.5 – Loop: until all attribute of element tag are read

5.5.1 – Start sub class of tag

5.5.2 – Write max cardinality restriction owl tag

5.5.3 – Write min cardinality restriction owl tag

5.5.4 – End sub class of tag

5.6 – End Loop   //starting from 5.5

5.7 – End class tag

6 – Loop: until all attributes of element tag are read

6.1 – Start property tag with reference ID named as attribute name

6.2 – Write isDefinedBy tag

6.3 – Write subPropertyOf tag

6.4 – Write label tag

6.5 – Write comment tag

6.6 – Write range tag

6.7 – Write domain tag

6.8 – close property tag

7 – End Loop   // Starting from 6

8 – End Loop	// Starting from 5
9 – Close RDF tag	
10 - End	

4.9.2.1 Data Flow diagram of Transformation

An abstract degree representation of conversion Procedure Is displayed in Figure 24 that points out a practice of transformation by XSD into RDF.

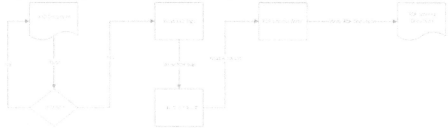

Figure 24: Transformation process of XSD to RDF Schema

4.9.2.2 Transformation of XML into RDF

Secondly, the stage of RDF Transformation would be to change the XML document to the RDF document soon after Schema conversion. In terms of uniformity, this conversion will be subdivided into two different activities, and you will always be to browse the XML document and keep ready conditions to alter to the RDF document in the second endeavour.

4.9.2.3 Reading XML File

XML document has been read, and data is automatically saved in ArrayList for short-term premise previously saving as RDF file. Initially, XML variant information is read out of XML Record as accomplished in XSD reading through. Right after reading through XML variant, XML schema tags have been read where merely a single piece of advice can observe, which identifies of father or mother name or element of the database. The component arrived after mydb component will be really for table title just as in between closing and opening of the desk tag, all features using values have been written. These worth pair will probably pay for you tuple price. It indicates that if you find just ten tuples at a desk afterwards, you can find just ten-value collections at that table label is started and shut ten instances.

4.9.2.4 Writing RDF File

They were written while composing the RDF schema file. From then on, the label is launched for table name for being a resource within the kind of world wide web connection as opposed to the shape of features. The finish will write relevance contrary feature of connection immediately after subsequent slash"/."

Exactly the Exact Same procedure is repeated till all of the worth from XML documents Are composed in ArrayList, which are by the ending offered to document writer composed in Java to publish RDF file as shown in Table 14.

Table 14: Reading XML and Writing RDF

1 – Write XML version tag

2 – Start RDF tag

    2.1 – Write RDF namespace

    2.2 – Write RDF schema namespace

    2.3 – Write OWL (Web Ontology Language) namespace

    2.4 – Write xmlns: Starter tag of XML= dummy_link where

        Dummy_link = http://www.MSThesis.IMS/mydb#

    2.5 – Close RDF tag

3 – Loop: until all records read from XML

    3.1 – Start description tag

    3.2 – rdf:about = dummy_link/XMLTag

    3.3 – Close description tag

    3.4 – Loop: until simple tag with complex are finished

        3.4.1 – Start tag starter tag of XML:Simple tag

        3.4.2 – rdf:resource = dummy_link/XML Simple tag value

        3.4.3 – close tag

    3.5 – End Loop   // Starting at 3.4

4 – End Loop   // Starting at 3

5 – Write closing RDF tag

6 - End

4.9.2.5 Flow chart diagram of the transformation

Out of XML document and saved at ArrayList, then an identical RDF document is already written. A flow graph with the transformation is connected, as shown in Figure 25.

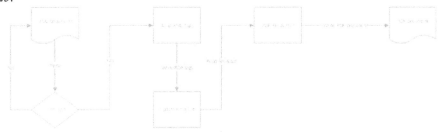

Figure 25: XML Transformation into RDF

4.10 Validation

It is a Significant Aspect of application technology to Examine the test and confirm which outcomes are arriving predicated to this condition. In our example, the undertaking would always be to produce ontologies/triples predicated on RDF. Thus, we must confirm/confirm that the records are generated. Thus, the records out there for empowerment are XSD (XML Schema file), XML document, RDF schema document along with RDF file. Thus, we broke up the identification procedure to two big categories, which are analysis of XML, and next is currently validation of RDF.

4.10.1 XML Files Validation

In thesis job investigation for XML documents, embraced two Techniques. The investigation is utilizing link supplied by W3C, and the moment is my java code.

4.10.2 XML Validation by Web Link

XML Schema and XML documents have been glued in the Hyperlink Http://www.utilities-online.info/xsdvalidation/#.VucbIZx97IU that encode the documents following W3C requirements. After available the connection, it reveals windows such as supplied under as shown in Figure 26; XSD (XML Schema) document is started and then glue it from the connection After restarting the XSD record, legitimacy assess Button is also pushed it exhibits the consequence of validation provided as shown in Figure 27.

Figure 26: XML and XSD validation web site

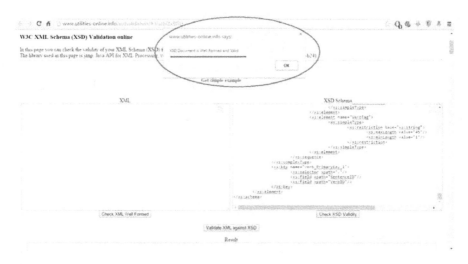

Figure 27: XSD validation Result

Later, XML code has been glued within the internet URL for affirmation and analysis based on W3C requirements. XML document is assessed by pressing on Verify XML very well click on link shape. The Result is revealed by Popup dividers concerning the validity of the XML document as shown in Figure 28.

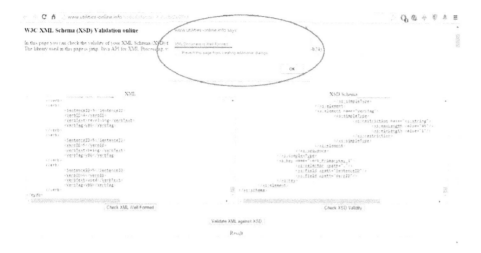

Figure 28: XML validation Result

After the two XSD and XML documents have been supported separately, today, it is the right time and energy to confirm XML from XSD. That is achieved just by pressing on a button off. Validate XML from XSD button can create effect against the investigation That's displayed in Figure 29 Connected beneath;

Sam-e identification can be made in a different Internet supply to Cross to assess the outcomes. Still, another tried web origin is http://www.freeformatter.com/xml-validator-xsd.html. Much like the instance explained previously, XML and XSD documents have been duplicated in the Writing place Provided on internet variant exhibited in Figure 30 and consequences of validations are displayed in Figure 31.

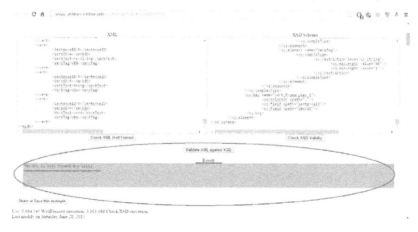

Figure 29: XML validation against XSD Result

There is no limit to the file you can upload but be patient with big or huge files.

XML Input

Option 1: Copy-paste your XML string here

```
            <SentenceID>5</SentenceID>
            <VerbID>6</VerbID>
            <VerbText>used</VerbText>
            <VerbTag>VBN</VerbTag>
        </verb>
    </mydb>
```

Option 2: Or type in the URL to your XML file

```
http://www.example.com/en/file.xml
```

XSD Input

Option 1: Copy-paste your XSD string here

```
                <xs:selector xpath="."/>
                <xs:field xpath="SentenceID"/>
                <xs:field xpath="VerbID"/>
            </xs:key>
        </xs:element>
    </xs:schema>
```

Option 2: Or type in the URL to your XSD file

```
```

VALIDATE XML

Figure 30: XML and XSD validation web site

XML Validator - XSD (XML Schema)

Validates the XML string/file against the specified XSD string/file. XSD files are "XML Schemas" that describe the structure of a XML document. The validator checks for well formedness first, meaning that your XML file must be parsable using a DOM/SAX parser, and only then does it validate your XML against the XML Schema. The validator will report fatal errors, non-fatal errors and warnings.

There is no limit to the file you can upload but be patient with big or huge files.

The XML document is fully valid.   Close

XML Input

Option 1: Copy-paste your XML string here

```
<?xml version="1.0" encoding="UTF-8"?>
<mydb xmlns:xs="http://www.w3.org/2001/XMLSchema" xmlns:xsi="http://www.w3.org/2001/XMLSchema-instance"
xsi:schemaLocation="http://www.w3schools.com XSD_output_mydb.xsd">
    <adjective>
        <SentenceID>4</SentenceID>
        <AdjectiveID>1</AdjectiveID>
```

Option 2: Or type in the URL to your XML file

```
http://www.example.com/en/file.xml
```

XSD Input

Option 1: Copy-paste your XSD string here

```
<?xml version="1.0" encoding="UTF-8"?>
<xs:schema xmlns:xs="http://www.w3.org/2001/XMLSchema" elementFormDefault="qualified" attributeFormDefault="unqualified">
<xs:element name="mydb">
<xs:complexType>
```

Figure 31: XML validation against XSD Result

4.10.3 XML Validation by Java Code

Still, another approach utilized to confirm XML documents (XML and XSD) code snippet is offered in Table 15 and Table 16 to mention.

Table 15: Java code for XML and XSD Validation function validator ()

```
public static void validator()
{
System.out.print("Start validating XSD and XML Files");
String fileXSD, fileXML;
fileXSD = "XSD_output_mydb.xsd";
fileXML = "XML_output_mydb.xml";
boolean isValid = validateXMLSchema(fileXSD, fileXML);
if(isValid){
 System.out.println("XML File \""+ fileXML + "\" is VALIDATED against XML
 Schema File\"" + fileXSD + "\"");}
else {
 System.out.println("XML File \""+ fileXML + "\" is NOT VALIDATED against XML
 Schema File\"" + fileXSD + "\"");}
 }
```

Table 16: Java code for XML and XSD Validation function validateXMLSchema
(XML-File, XSD-File)

```
public static boolean validateXMLSchema(String xsdPath. String xmlPath)
{
try
{
SchemaFactory factory =
SchemaFactory.newInstance(XMLConstants.W3C_XML_SCHEMA_NS_URI);
Schema schema = factory.newSchema(new File(xsdPath)):
Validator validator = schema.newValidator():
validator.validate(new StreamSource(new File(xmlPath))):
}
catch (IOException e)
{
System.out.println("Exception: "+e.getMessage()):
return false:
}
catch(SAXException e1){
System.out.println("SAX Exception: "+e1.getMessage()):
return false:
}
return true:
}
```

Validate XML schema Work takes the records as input parameters to assess files single ability and alongside each other. Psychotherapy is thr by coffee in case any course of action encounters a mistake (therefore). The function yields a boolean value as one or zero. If data files have been verified afterwards, one price is returned no is returned. The following Procedure Is also displayed using all the aid stream diagram supplied under as Figure 32.

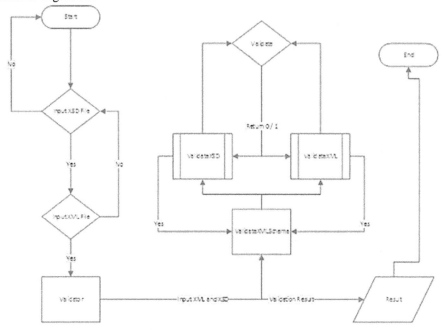

Figure 32: Validation Process XML and XSD

4.10.4 RDF Files Validation

In thesis job investigation for RDF data files employed with one procedure, that's validation by way of link. RDF Schema and RDF documents are clicked individually to have confirmed by link. That's https://www.w3.org/RDF/Validator/. RDF Schema document is text and copied is automatically glued about the Shape of Link offered over for analysis. A Screenshot Is Put beneath to Demonstrate that the glued RDF Schema ahead. RDF Schema document is text and copied Is glued around the shape of web-link offered over for analysis. A Screenshot Is Put beneath to Demonstrate that the glued RDF Schema ahead of supporting it as shown in Figure 33.

76

Figure 33 RDF text view before parsing

After pressing on parse RDF button together with choices of Triples along with Graph and place the output of charts such as PNG, GIF, etc., and the most RDF parser obtainable online will emphasize the RDF Schema text glued into emphasized text section at Figure 34. Results got to come at the shape of the triples along with the chart. Graph connection can be found to download in your computers. An Example outcome comprising an identification of RDF Schema and triples shaped is supplied under in Figure 35.

Figure 34 RDF Schema Validation and Triples

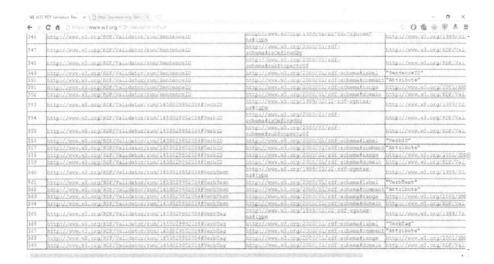

Figure 35 RDF Triples

You will find at complete 369 triples are created in Opposition to RDF Schema. Triples are revealed at the Shape of Matter, Predicate, and Object. Much like previously, the RDF document can also be input from the Sort of internet Established validator. Once parsing/verifying the same document type of effect will be staying generated that exhibits the validity of the RDF document along with the creation of triples. A sample output signal of RDF document parsing utilizing https://www.w3.org/RDF/Validator is Offered under Figure 36 to reveal outcomes of identification and triples creation.

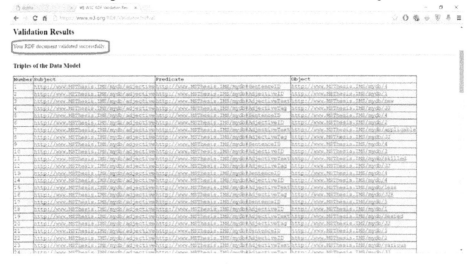

Figure 36 RDF Validation and Triples

4.11 RDF Graph

Graphs are made by just two approaches to reveal two different Forms of chart representation. One can be made by on-line web validator along with Second is via way of a visualization device to picture the RDF triple chart.

4.11.1 RDF Triple Graph by web

After RDF file input for validation/parsing, in case the document is confirmed, then the parser will make triples and chart predicated on to generated triples. We've got selections to conserve charts in various formats, which can be SVG, GIF, PNG, PostScript, and HPGL, which will be embedded within a webpage or can supply a URL to put in it. A sample chart to get RDF Schema revealed in. SVG document arrangement is displayed below as Figure 37 to Figure 39.

Figure 37 RDF Schema Triple Graph - 1

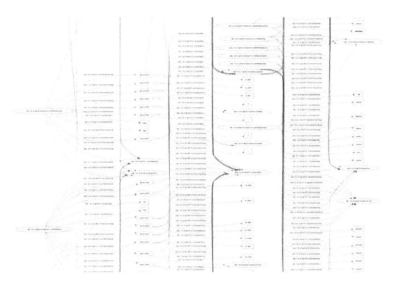

Figure 38 RDF Schema Triple Graph – 2

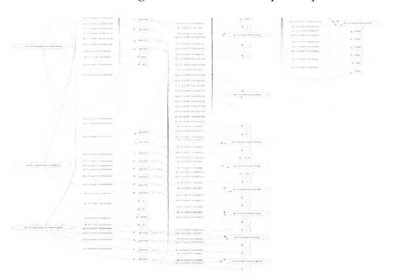

Figure 39 RDF Schema Triple Graph – 3

As triple created is overly much time to reveal to a single webpage. S O for revealing output signal of RDF document, a handful of worth have been shot by modifying the RDF file. The evaluation output signal of the triple chart is revealed in Figure 40.

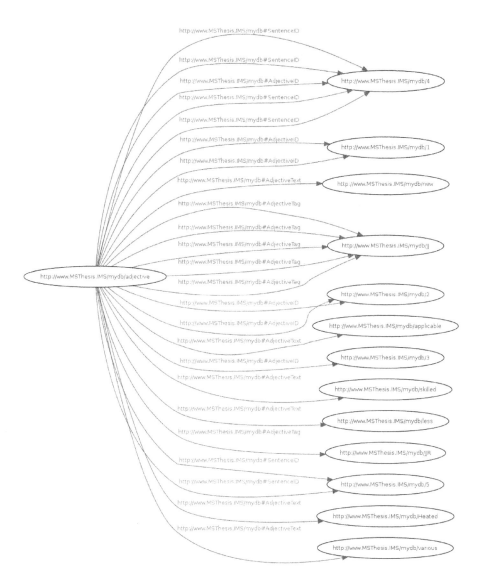

Figure 40 RDF Triple Graph

4.11.2 RDF Triple Graph by RDF Gravity

Secondly, embraced to Build an RDF triple chart is using an Extensively visualization instrument that's RDF Gravity. Back in RDF Gravity, the RDF document is entered from the package deal to build a triple chart also, and it lets to hunt the chart by feature/values or directory within chart combined side rescue the chart possibilities in most images file formats. RDF Gravity will just crank out the chart in the case entered

81

is supported the way it follows the W3C expectations. In case it doesn't, the chart of RDF won't be produced. Sample RDF triple charts to get RDF Schema and RDF, which are made by RDF gravity has been attached to demonstrate the second representation of chart triples, as shown in Figure 41 to Figure 43.

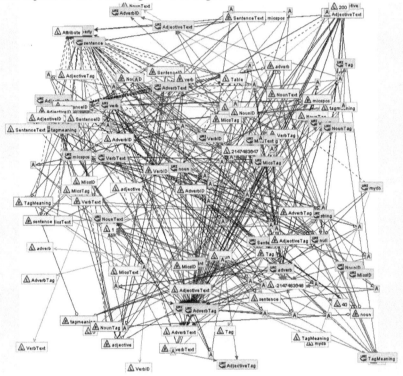

Figure 41 RDF Schema Graph generated by RDF Gravity

Figure 42 Simple RDF Graph generated by RDF Gravity

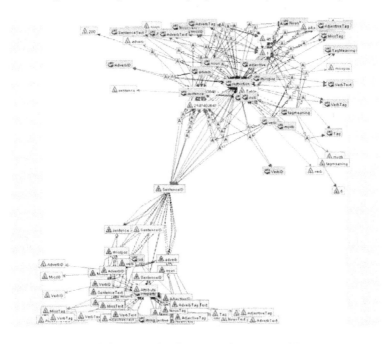

Figure 43 RDF Schema and values Graph generated by RDF Gravity

4.12 Conclusion, Limitations and Future Work

This analysis will probably help to Become regular conversions of text into ontologies// RDF triples. Even though a great deal of work carried out in this respect, however, one solution isn't found that can be able to offer one proceed surgery. This analysis has been expected to become standard in NLP/Semantic Internet niche eventually. As our means of changing information D B to XML and RDF will not rely upon the database, and thus virtually any database using understood statistics classes might be catered by the suggested approach to receive conventional conversions invented by the internet Consortium (W3C). This analysis, we now invented a mechanism to ease in subsequent step-by-step procedure in the direction of organizational internet production. An adaptive mechanism can be employed to transform Stanford parser came back tags (SynSets from WordNet) into a relational database. Even though, these tags may likewise be kept using document. But right here, we've experimented with to benefit from relational DB storage and indexing procedures rather than inventing our personal. Getting tags, text after which saving D B worth is completed by Jade brokers (java-based representatives) that'll behave as collaborative representatives. Right after such conversion that was implemented, D B established principles have been utilized to transform to extensible Markup Language according-to World Wide Web Consortium (W3C) criteria. It'll let us access D B data, which will be in each machine and human-readable structure. XML transformation is followed closely by RDF transformation. Assessing XML and XSD into source Description Framework (RDF) is a focused task of the thesis analysis to change an easy text to the directory successfully. These net-tools may also be called ontologies defined as raw information to get world wide web semantics.

As label/Synsets Transformation relies on processes From Stanford Parser, therefore we jump to adapt limitations with the package utilized by WordNet. We assumed to be more certain about syntax and semantics of text because WordNet// Stanford Parser would maybe not revolve, until that moment. In case we're speaking about great things about using brokers, then it's maybe not up into the sense of this marker to accomplishing parallelism and finding out collaborative representatives. In the transformation of input into DB, XML, and RDF, we just contemplated well-known datatypes. Therefore, it's likewise much feasible to become a flaw, maybe not to manage strange statistics types like a BLOB.

This exploration will probably invent a way to transform WordNet (huge lexical database of English speech) Synsets to RDF triples. RDF triples act as raw information into inventing ontologies. Our upcoming job will center over a measure of progress to shape ontologies. The following part of the mind would be it to create multi-agents that may not just keep in touch together but additionally helps form a system established collaborative representatives are working. Handling information sorts that aren't ordinarily utilized at Relational DB, we could mould our extent to create an option in conditions of coordinated treatment to access big-data representation to conventional web tools.

5 CONSTRUCTS AND MAPPING FOR RDB, XML, AND RDF

5.1 Overview

Online programs usually store Relational Database Shape (RDB) details or Summary of Resources (RDF) details. The knowledge has to be transferred to the next kind in 1 class. There are some conversion methods, but there are no strong performance issues. Also, the Literature clarifies numerous rigid approaches, with data loss and restricted personalization, for conversion from RDB to RDF. This technique does not utilize an alternative form to avoid either of these data forms consistency issues. This paper has a whole new methodology that enables data analysis to be carried out. This mapping is used to explain their differences in the degree of representation of knowledge (ALoufi et al., 2019). The mapping can be done with the interim knowledge recorder Extensible Markup Language (XML). This technique often permits the two-way transfer of data from RDB along with RDF without data reduction through knowledge grasp. In almost any modification of the records, that is a means to upgrade the dilemma. Conventional approaches may, however, be adapted to the methodology developed by the Semantic Internet. The same happens as data is transferred directly back to DB. This two-way conversion does not result in a drop in knowledge, which provides continuity between traditional and specific data forms. It will encourage one to use inference and logic for unconventional processes.

5.2 Generic Constructs for RDB, XML, and RDF

5.2.1 XML Structure

```
1   <?xml version="1.0" encoding="UTF-8"?>
2   <xs:schema xmlns:xs="http://www.w3.org/2001/XMLSchema"
3   elementFormDefault="qualified" attributeFormDefault="unqualified">
4   <xs:element name="Database-Name">
5   <xs:complexType>
6   <xs:sequence>
7   <xs:element ref="Table-Name" minOccurs = "0" maxOccurs = "unbounded" />
8   </xs:sequence>
9   </xs:complexType>
10  </xs:element>
11      <xs:element name="Table-Name">
12          <xs:complexType>
13              <xs:sequence>
14                  <xs:element name="Field-Name">
15                      <xs:simpleType>
16                          <xs:restriction base="datatype">
17                              <xs:minInclusive value="Minimum-Size"/>
18                              <xs:maxInclusive value="Maximum-Size"/>
19                          </xs:restriction>
20                      </xs:simpleType>
21                  </xs:element>
22                  <xs:element ref="Reference-Field-Name" minOccurs="0" maxOccurs="unbounded"/>
23              </xs:sequence>
24          </xs:complexType>
```

```
25    <xs:key name="Unique-Identifier-Code">
26        <xs:selector xpath="."/>
27        <xs:field xpath="Unique-Identifier-Field-Name"/>
28    </xs:key>
29    <xs:keyref name="Reference-Identifier-Code" refer="Unique-Identifier-Code">
30        <xs:selector xpath="Reference-Table-Name"/>
31        <xs:field xpath="Reference-Field-Name"/>
32    </xs:keyref>
33   </xs:element>
34 </xs:schema>
```

5.2.2 XML Structure

```
1  <?xml version="1.0" encoding="UTF-8"?>
2  <Database-Name xmlns:xs="http://www.w3.org/2001/XMLSchema"
3  xmlns:xsi="http://www.w3.org/2001/XMLSchema-instance"
4  xsi:schemaLocation="Drive://Directory-Location">
5      <Table-Name>
6          <Field-Name>Value</Field-Name>
7      </Table-Name>
8  </Database-Name>
```

5.2.3 RDFS Structure

```
1  <?xml version='1.0' encoding='ISO-8859-1'?>
2  <rdf:RDF
3  xmlns:rdf="http://www.w3.org/1999/02/22-rdf-syntax-ns#"
4  xmlns:rdfs="http://www.w3.org/2000/01/rdf-schema#"
5  xmlns:owl="http://www.w3.org/2002/07/owl#" >
6      <rdfs:Class rdf:about="Table-Name">
7          <rdfs:label>Table-Name</rdfs:label>
8          <rdfs:comment>Table</rdfs:comment>
9          <rdfs:subClassOf rdf:resource="Database-Name"/>
10         <rdfs:subClassOf>
11             <owl:restriction>
12                 <owl:onProperty rdf:resource="Field-Name" />
13                 <owl:minCardinality rdf:datatype="&xsd;nonNegativeInteger">
14                 Minimum-Size</owl:minCardinality>
15             </owl:restriction>
16         </rdfs:subClassOf>
17         <rdfs:subClassOf>
18             <owl:restriction>
19                 <owl:onProperty rdf:resource="Field-Name" />
20                 <owl:maxCardinality rdf:datatype="&xsd;nonNegativeInteger">
21                 Maximum-Size</owl:maxCardinality>
22             </owl:restriction>
23         </rdfs:subClassOf>
24     </rdfs:Class>
```

5.2.4 A Property

```
25   ┌  <rdf:Property rdf:about="Field-Name">
26   │      <rdfs:isDefinedBy rdf:resource="Table-Name/Reference-Identifier-Table-Name"/>
27   │      <rdfs:subPropertyOf rdf:resource="Unique-Identifier-Field-Name/Reference-Identifier-Field-Name"/>
28   │      <rdfs:label>Field-Name</rdfs:label>
29   │      <rdfs:comment>Attribute</rdfs:comment>
30   │      <rdfs:range rdf:resource="datatype"/>
31   │      <rdfs:domain rdf:resource="Table-Name"/>
32   └  </rdf:Property>
33   └</rdf:RDF>
```

5.2.5 RDF Structure

```
1    <?xml version='1.0' encoding='ISO-8859-1'?>
2    <rdf:RDF
3    xmlns:rdf="http://www.w3.org/1999/02/22-rdf-syntax-ns#"
4    xmlns:rdfs="http://www.w3.org/2000/01/rdf-schema#"
5   ┌xmlns:owl="http://www.w3.org/2002/07/owl#">
6   ├    <rdf:Description rdf:about="Table-Name">
7   │        <Database-Name:Field-Name>Value</Database-Name:Field-Name>
8   ├    </rdf:Description>
9   └</rdf:RDF>
```

5.3 Improving Data Mapping

To conquer these problems shared in the preceding portion of information investigation, brand new, and other data representations must be properly used. To such lavish throughout conversion procedure intermediate terminology since XML can be used owing to the common use and personalization capacities. Mapping of Relational Schema, XML Schema, also RDFS has been awarded in Table 17. Whereby each theory regarding, statistics are represented so in procuring supported and a better link between information transformation.

Table 17: Mapping of the Concepts Similarities of Languages

Concepts	Relational Schema	XML Schema	RDFS
Table	Table_Name	Complex type element	rdfs:Class
Field	Field_Name	Simple Element	RDF: Property
Cardinality	Min	xs:restriction xs:minLength or xs:minInclusive	owl:restriction owl:minCardinality
Cardinality	Max	xs:restriction xs:minLength or xs:minInclusive	owl:restriction owl:maxCardinality
Referencing	Ref_Key_Field Ref_Key_Table	xs:keyref xs:selector and xs:field	rdfs:domain rdfs:isDefinedBy
Primary Key	Key_Field	xs:key	rdfs:subPropertyOf

		xs:selector and xs:field	rdfs:isDefinedBy
Composite key	Key_Fields	xs:key xs:selector and xs:field	(P) Embedded in RDF's:subPropertyOf
Data type	Datatype	xs:restriction base	rdfs:range

5.4 The mapping between XML data for Both Sides During Transformation

Mapping strategy would always be to follow along XML Generated data obtained from RDB or even RDF throughout the method after bi-directional information Transformation type. Identification of shift eventually becomes radically simple as they can certainly be understood by studying just two of those cases, including importance shift and brand-new subject embedded into the information. Let us have the very first ever to observe that the happening if a brand-new field becomes inserted in the RDF information (Malik et al., 2018b). In Figure 44, it's demonstrated a discipline termed "father name" has been inserted from the RDF data. It can be dependent upon distributing XML data files at enough full-time foundations. After the diagnosis of altering incident, a fresh land goes to be inserted from the RDFS record of their machine information.

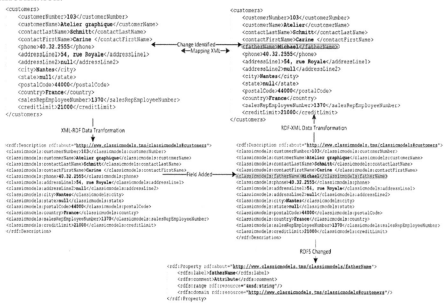

Figure 44: Mapping of XML files shows an update needed in RDF Schema to record any change

Still another, the event of altering seen at the worthiness such as the title area worth in RDF has been shifted out of "Atelier Graphique" to" Atelier" as shown in Figure 45. This shift may likewise be detected, having a mapping in the degree of all XML data files time coming from RDB later conversion. Such a change demanded simply to upgrade exactly the other hand of this information origin at which this instance is RDB discipline "identify" underneath the connection "clients" for its listing of ID "10 3". This shift isn't hard to take care of; however, in the previous instance, handling switch could cause upgrade anomalies to arise. And demands careful management of their information and metadata upgrades to quantify will be affected data and fields in case any.

Figure 45: Mapping of XML data to record any change of data

5.5   Functions for Mapping Data

The modelling of this post begins with placing a flag. Find features in RDF, and also RDB is exactly the not. Subsequently, information is spelt with operating MD () using debate of XML file acquired from RDF or RDB and assessed whether worth, in conclusion, is merged if altered up to intermediate information structure.

$$flag = \begin{cases} false & if\ L_i(t) = L_j(t)\ and\ flag = false \\ true & if\ L_i(t) \neq L_j(t) \end{cases} \tag{1}$$

$$MD(XML_{RDB}) = \begin{cases} 0 & if\ L_i(t) = L_i(t')\ or\ flag = false \\ 1 & if\ L_i(t) \neq L_i(t') \end{cases} \tag{2}$$

$$MD(XML_{RDF}) = \begin{cases} 0 & if\ L_j(t) = L_j(t')\ or\ flag = false \\ 1 & if\ L_j(t) \neq L_j(t') \end{cases} \tag{3}$$

$$\therefore 1 \le i \le n \, and \, 1 \le j \le m \ni n, m \in +\square \, , L_i \in XSD_{RDB}, L_j \in XSD_{RDF} \, and \, t, t' \in time$$

By Employing Eq. 1 to reveal worth in RDB and also RDF Set to get the same list example are the same or perhaps not. In Eq. 3 and 2 two Mapping purposes are utilized to compute a case worth at time t even equals precisely the same significance at the preceding moment Using the Aid of Eq. 6, 5 7, and 7 Can get collected matrix for calculating mapping of info where L shaped per listing of Features within a DB currently found possibly in RDB or even RDF facet of the platform holding information From XML data files. The resultant equation of a matrix CSVMD, which is obtained from the data level mapping between XML files, is sh in Where Eq. (4) as shown in Table 18.

$$CSV_{MD} = \bigcup_{e=1}^{p} \left(MD((XML_{RDB})_e) + MD((XML_{RDF})_e) \right) \tag{4}$$

Table 18 Comparing BDTM with Other Transformation Languages

Features	R2O (2002)	D2RQ (2004)	Relational.OWL (2005)	Virtuoso (2007)	Triplify (2009)	R3M (2010)	R2RML (2012)	Direct Mapping (2012)	D2RQ/Update (2012)	BDTM (2016)
Relation to Class	✓	✓	☑	✓	✓	☑	✓	☑	✓	✓
Update	✗	✗	✗	✗	✗	☑	✗	✗	✗	✓
Record URI	✓	✓	✗	✓	✓	✓	✓	✗	✓	✓
Data Reuse	✗	✗	✗	✗	✗	✗	✗	✗	✗	✓
Datatypes	✓	✓	✓	✓	✓	✓	✓	✗	✓	✓
Integrity Constraints	☑	☑	☑	☑	☑	✓	☑	✗	☑	✓
Write Support	✗	✗	✓	✗	✗	✓	✗	✓	☑	✓
Data Transformation	✓	✓	☒	☒	✓	✓	✓	✓	✓	✓
Query base Transformation	✓	✓	✗	✓	✓	✓	✓	✗	✓	☑
Bidirectional Transformation	✗	✗	✗	✗	✗	☑	✗	✗	✗	✓

Legends:

✓ Supported feature
✗ Not Supported feature
☑ Partial Support of feature
☒ Unknown

6   TOOLS AND APPLICATIONS

Heritage of XML begins in 1996 With all the addition of XML variant 1.0 from Tim Bray. XPath can be utilized to browse utilizing the XML file thing. XSLT model 1.0 and XPath model 1.0 gave tips from 1999 to the benchmark. Back in 2001, XML Schema was appointed as an excuse. And upgrade to XML Schema had been launched in 2004. This background proceeds and information could be viewed following this deadline in Table 19. XSLT-based alter is an excellent Outline of the syntactic reversal of XML information. For the context, XSLT can be utilized for the civic switch in between unique XML-designs, e.g., XPATH2 expressions certainly are similarly a potential strategy. Each record of the specific benchmark is shifted to a looking at recognized architecture in the middle of the modified phonetic period. XPath is a language used to pinpoint accurate XML nodes at a DOM. And now XQuery is a superset of XPath, which likewise supplies FLWOR syntax that will be SQL-like.

Table 19: Historical Evolution of XML

| Timeline | | Extensible Markup Language (XML) | | | | | |
| | | Introduced | | | Standardized | | |
Sr.	Year	Author	Description	Key Term	Author	Description	Key Term
1	Nov. 1996	[Tim Bray, et al., Nov. 1996]	Extensible Markup Language (XML)	XML 1.0	-	-	-
2	Aug. 1998	[James Clark, et al., Aug. 1998]	Extensible Stylesheet Language (XSL) Version 1.0	XSLT 1.0	-	-	-
3	Jul. 1999	[James Clark, et al., Jul. 1999]	XML Path Language (XPath) Version 1.0	XPATH 1.0	-	-	-
4	Nov. 1999	-	-	-	[James Clark, et al., Nov. 1999]	XSL Transformations (XSLT) Version 1.0	XSLT 1.0
5	Nov. 1999	-	-	-	[James Clark, et al., Nov. 1999]	XML Path Language (XPath) Version 1.0	XPATH 1.0

6	Feb. 2000	[David C. Fallside, Feb. 2000]	XML Schema Part 0: Primer	XML Schema 1.0	-	-	-
7	Feb. 2001	[Don Chamberlin, et al., Feb. 2001]	XQuery: A Query Language for XML	XQuery 1.0	-	-	-
8	May. 2001	-	-	-	[David C. Fallside, May. 2001]	XML Schema Part 0: Primer	XML Schema 1.0
9	Dec. 2001	[John Cowan, Dec. 2001]	XML Blueberry (XML 1.1)	XML 1.1	-	-	-
10	Dec. 2001	[Michael Kay, Jan. 2007]	XSL Transformations (XSLT) Version 2.0	XSLT 2.0	-	-	-
11	Dec. 2001	[Anders Berglund, et al., Dec. 2001]	XML Path Language (XPath) 2.0	XPATH 2.0	-	-	-
12	Jul. 2004	[Henry S. Thompson, et al., Jul. 2004] & [David Peterson, et al., Jul. 2004]	XML Schema 1.1 Part 1: Structures & XML Schema 1.1 Part 2: Datatypes	XML Schema 1.1	-	-	-
13	Jul. 2004	[Sihem Amer-Yahia, et al., Jul. 2004]	XQuery 1.0 and XPath 2.0 Full-Text	XQuery & XPath Full-Text	-	-	-
14	Jan. 2006	[Don Chamberlin, et al., Jan. 2006]	XQuery Update Facility	XQuery Update	-	-	-
15	Aug. 2006	-	-	-	[Tim Bray, et al., Aug. 2006]	Extensible Markup Language (XML) 1.0 (Fourth Edition)	XML 1.0

16	Aug. 2006	-	-	-	[Tim Bray, et al., Aug. 2006]	Extensible Markup Language (XML) 1.1 (Second Edition)	XML 1.1
17	Jan. 2007	-	-	-	[Scott Boag, et al., Jan. 2007]	XQuery 1.0: An XML Query Language	XQuery 1.0
18	Jan. 2007	-	-	-	[Anders Berglund, et al., Jan. 2007]	XML Path Language (XPath) 2.0	XPATH 2.0
19	Jan. 2007	-	-	-	[Michael Kay, Jan. 2007]	XSL Transformations (XSLT) Version 2.0	XSLT 2.0
20	Jul. 2008	[Don Chamberlin, et al., Jul. 2008]	XQuery 1.1: An XML Query Language	XQuery 1.1	-	-	-
21	Dec. 2010	[Jonathan Robie, et al., Dec. 2010]	XQuery 3.0: An XML Query Language	XQuery 3.0	-	-	-
22	Dec. 2010	[Jonathan Robie, et al., Dec. 2010]	XML Path Language (XPath) 3.0	XPath 3.0	-	-	-
22	Mar. 2011	-	-	-	[Pat Case, et al., Mar. 2011]	XQuery and XPath Full Text 1.0	XQuery and XPath Full Text 1.0
23	Mar. 2011	-	-	-	[Jonathan Robie, et al., Mar. 2011]	XQuery Update Facility 1.0	XQuery Update
24	Dec. 2011	[Mary Holstege, et al., Dec. 2011]	XQuery and XPath Full Text 3.0	XQuery and XPath Full Text 3.0	-	-	-

25	Jul. 2012	[Michael Kay, Jul. 2012]	XSL Transformations (XSLT) Version 3.0	XSLT 3.0	-	-	-
26	Apr. 2012	-	-	-	[Henry S. Thompson, et al., Apr. 2012] & [David Peterson, et al., Apr. 2012]	W3C XML Schema Definition Language (XSD) 1.1 Part 1: Structures & W3C XML Schema Definition Language (XSD) 1.1 Part 2: Datatypes	XML Schema 1.1
27	Apr. 2014	-	-	-	[Jonathan Robie, et al., Apr. 2014]	XQuery 3.0: An XML Query Language	XQuery 3.0
28	Apr. 2014	-	-	-	[Jonathan Robie, et al., Apr. 2014]	XML Path Language (XPath) 3.0	XPath 3.0
29	Nov. 2015	-	-	-	[Mary Holstege, et al., Nov. 2015]	XQuery and XPath Full Text 3.0	XQuery and XPath Full Text 3.0

Next Figure 46 shows the XML information version report development separately revealing when just about every theory and their upgrades had been introduced along with once they've been manufactured standardized. In the beginning, the thought of the construction with the capacity of use was launched, and if it had been older, afterwards, it turned into a suggestion to serve as a benchmark as shown in Figure 47.

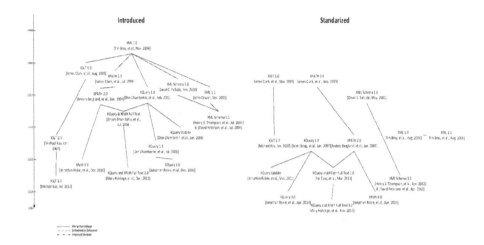

Figure 46: Depiction of XML data model evolution history separately showing when were introduced and when were standardized. Back in Figure 2-4, Rating of XML is exhibited with their tips of W3C together linking them through traces in line with this deadline in the face of the body to demonstrate their birth year-wise in line with this historical past. Currently, the following section ancient test of RDF information version is symbolized.

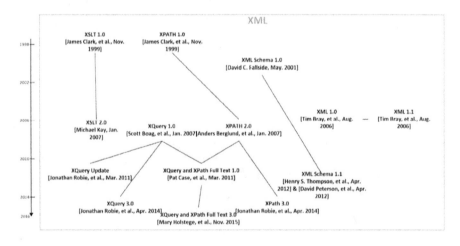

Figure 47: History of XML data model standardization evolution

6.1 Resource Description Framework (RDF)

The RDF is owned by the household of Standards invented by W3C. Even the W3C company was doing work on presenting data that was linked and making it utilized like a benchmark for information to be reflected in the shape of triples. Attractive attributes of RDF comprise the mixing of information if interior schemas disagree, plus its change elastic character. RDF is currently widely useful for symbolizing web funds within the sort of Profession description. Also, it's its usage in expertise management methods. Whereas RDF Schema aids in establishing a base for RDF metadata also, it supplies interoperability involving dispersed and different processes about information representation and understandability such as devices. Heritage of RDF Schema Specs Utilized for specifying RDF construction with semantics premiered in March 1999. At the same time, the information representation in RDF kind called RDF Primer was released in March 2002. About July 2002, characteristic synopsis for both OWL Lite and OWL had been launched. OWL two Prime changed variant of OWL premiered April 2008 and has been created normally in October 2009. Likewise, advancements had been manufactured from SPARQL since SPARQL 1.1 in Oct 2009, and so were created normally in March 2013. RDF has been first modified in August 2011 since RDF 1.1 and RDF a was created normally in June 2011. RDB into RDF programming speech R2RML was released in October 2010 and has been made being a normal speech of communicating in September 2012. Changes in such theories, regulations, and specifications remain going right through the procedure of developments. The Time-wise description of data associated with RDF information version history development has been awarded in Table 20. Additional background following this calendar year 2014 to get RDF isn't covered as W3C" RDF Working team" is working on developments worried about the RDF information version.

Table 20: Historical Evolution of RDF

Timeline		Resource Description Framework (RDF)					
		Introduced			Standardized		
Sr.	Yea r	Author	Description	Key Term	Author	Descriptio n	Key Term
1	Mar. 199 9	[Dan Brickley et al., Mar. 1999]	Resource Description Framework (RDF) Schema Specificatio n	RDF Schema	-	-	-
2	Mar. 200 2	[Frank Manola, et al., Mar 2002]	RDF Primer	RDF	-	-	-
3	Jul. 200 2	[Deborah L. McGuinness et al., Jul. 2002]	Feature Synopsis for	OWL	-	-	-

			OWL Lite and OWL				
4	Feb. 200 4	-	-	-	[Dan Brickley, et al., Feb. 2004]	RDF Vocabular y Descriptio n Language 1.0: RDF Schema	RDF Schema
5	Feb. 200 4	-	-	-	[Frank Manola, et al., Feb 2004]	RDF Primer	RDF
6	Feb. 200 4	-	-	-	[Deborah L. McGuinness, et al., Feb. 2004]	OWL Web Ontology Language Overview	OWL
7	Oct. 200 4	[Eric Prud'hommeau x, et al., Oct. 2004]	SPARQL Query Language for RDF	SPARQ L	-	-	-
8	Oct. 200 7	[Ben Adida, et al. Oct. 2007]	RDFa in XHTML: Syntax and Processing - A collection of attributes and processing rules for extending XHTML to support RDF	RDFa	-	-	-
9	Jan. 200 8	-	-	-	[Eric Prud'hommeau x, et al., Jan. 2008]	SPARQL Query Language for RDF	SPARQ L
	Apr. 200 8	[Bijan Parsia, et al., Apr. 2008]	OWL 2 Web Ontology Language: Primer	OWL 2	-	-	-

10	Oct. 200 8	-	-	-	[Ben Adida, et al. Oct. 2008]	RDFa in XHTML: Syntax and Processing - A collection of attributes and processing rules for extending XHTML to support RDF	RDFa
11	Oct. 200 9	[Steve Harris et al., Oct. 2009]	SPARQL 1.1 Query Language	SPARQ L 1.1	-	-	-
12	Oct. 200 9	-	-	-	[Pascal Hitzler, et al., Oct. 2009]	OWL 2 Web Ontology Language Primer	OWL 2
13	Apr. 201 0	[Ben Adida et al., Apr. 2010]	RDFa Core 1.1 - Syntax and processing rules for embedding RDF through attributes	RDFa Core 1.1	-	-	-
14	Oct. 201 0	[Souripriya Das, et al., Oct. 2010]	R2RML: RDB to RDF Mapping Language	R2RML	-	-	-
15	Aug . 201 1	[Richard Cyganiak, et al., Aug. 2011]	RDF 1.1 Concepts and Abstract Syntax	RDF 1.1	-	-	-

16	Jun. 2012	-	-	-	[Ben Adida et al., Jun. 2012]	RDFa Core 1.1 - Syntax and processing rules for embedding RDF through attributes	RDFa Core 1.1
17	Sep. 2012	-	-	-	[Souripriya Das, et al., Sep. 2012]	R2RML: RDB to RDF Mapping Language	R2RML
18	Mar. 2013	-	-	-	[Steve Harris, et al., Mar. 2013]	SPARQL 1.1 Query Language	SPARQL 1.1
19	Jan. 2014	[Dan Brickley, et al., Jan. 2014]	Data-modelling vocabulary for RDF data	RDF Schema 1.1	-	-	-
20	Feb. 2014	-	-	-	[Richard Cyganiak, et al., Feb. 2014]	RDF 1.1 Concepts and Abstract Syntax	RDF 1.1
21	Feb. 2014	-	-	-	[Dan Brickley, et al., Feb. 2014]	Data-modelling vocabulary for RDF data	RDF Schema 1.1

Next, Figure 48 depicts RDF information version background development separately revealing when every theory and their upgrades were released along with if they had been created standardized. In the beginning, the thought of the construction with the capacity of used was launched, and also, if it had been older, afterwards, it turned into a suggestion to function as a benchmark.

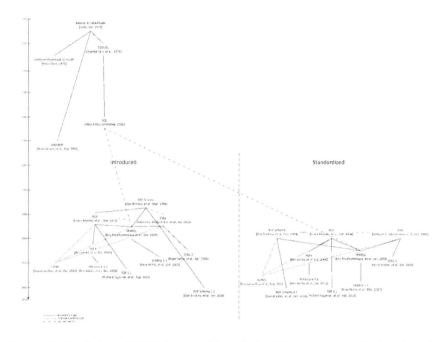

Figure 48: Depiction of RDF data model evolution history separately showing when were introduced and when were standardized

Back in Figure 49, analysis of RDF is revealed with their recommendations of W3C together linking them collectively through traces based on this deadline in the facet of their body to reveal their birth year-wise based on this background.

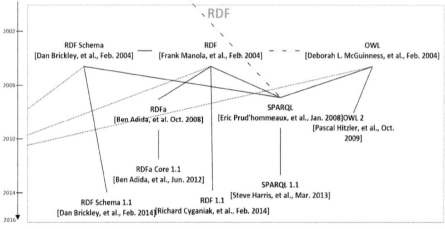

Figure 49: History of RDF data model standardization evolution

6.2 Comparison between different Platforms, and Languages

Once studying the development of distinct data units today, we evaluate various languages, tools, and programs utilized for changing information and metadata amongst RDB and RDF. Heritage of programming speech deadline wise reflected in cerebral Start-S from 2003 to 2012 comprising state-of-the-art platforms and languages such as data conversion amongst RDB along with RDF. They've launched mapping from the shape of manual, direct, and language-based ways for RDB and RDF, and sometimes even a few have even sh lengthy bi-directional data conversion utilizing the question-oriented procedure. Now to view that which platform or language is given a greater way for information conversion without even sacrificing some essential information regarding information by specifying them individually and temporarily. And farther assessing for comprehending capacities in the encouraging characteristics for information conversion procedure.

One of the mapping languages offered in Table 21 short introduction of every launch with Immediate Mapping that supplies an immediate mechanism to convert RDBs to Semantic Internet by mapping table class and field. In comparison, RDB schemes and statistics mechanically generate URIs. R2O was intended with very low similarity to handle complicated mapping in RDFS or OWL ontologies with self-improvement results. Return to reference. OWL, OWL The structure and statistical details of an RDB are mainly focused on ontological representation. Open Connect Program offers RDF Viewpoints that show similar knowledge around the Semantic Net. A host recognized as Virtuoso Universal Server. The data collection extracted from a database may be represented by a SQL Pick query in a few times as long. In comparison, SQL DDL produces an aspect of opinion syntax degree. D2RQ may be used to transform pre-defined RDB data into graphical RDF diagrams. Where access is given by SPARQL inquiries and related details to the Semantic Internet knowledge. Undefined translation of RDB to RDF notifications may be query-oriented to dispense related details from RDB. Related details from RDBs. Triplify was rendered with PHP scripts/code. transformation. The W3C proposal to translate the structured RDB approach into RDF translation was created by R2RML, a mapping expression. A conversion speech named R3 M was added during the access mediation point. It enables selective, two-way, question-oriented, RDF-oriented touch to the RDB as an update and cautious transfer language.

In this sub-section, various small improvements and resources were exchanged to pay for the warmest research on the conversion process. Sheet2RDF (2015), after a process of immediate mapping, can be the tool which transforms knowledge out of the dictionary in three RDF files. It neglects to recognize the option to schemes. A subsequent semi-automation may be introduced as Ultrawrap Mapper (2015) for RDB mapping to RDF with the R2RML script. RDF(S)-OWL (2016) meets Instant Mapping and R2RML improvements to the ontology RDB Schema. This role is based strongly on the dissemination of rules on the conversion process.

Table 21: Comparison between different Transformation Platforms, Tools and Languages

Features	R2O (2002)	D2RQ (2004)	Relational. OWL (2005)	Virtuoso (2007)	Triplify (2009)	R3M (2010)	R2RML (2012)	Direct Mapping (2012)	D2RQ/Update (2012)
Relation to Class	□	□	□	□	□	□	□	□	□
Update	□	□	□	□	□	□	□	□	□
Record URI	□	□	□	□	□	□	□	□	□
Data Reuse	□	□	□	□	□	□	□	□	□
Datatypes	□	□	□	□	□	□	□	□	□
Integrity Constraints	□	□	□	□	□	□	□	□	□
Write Support	□	□	□	□	□	□	□	□	□
Data Transformation	□	□	□	□	□	□	□	□	□
Query base Transformation	□	□	□	□	□	□	□	□	□
Bidirectional Transformation	□	□	□	□	□	□	□	□	□

The symbol □ represents supported features; the symbol □ represents not supported features; the symbol □ represents partially supported features; the symbol □ represents unknown features.

The challenge in upgrading RDB and RDF details on either side is worried as it is expected to update. The reuse of data involves problems that may be done for almost any provided source when utilizing XML-made data. Although it supports writing-only D2RQ/Update in RDF retail shop, maybe it doesn't help RDB. Returning to Table 2-3 all attributes are described, such as terminology, update, URI, knowledge reuse, data forms, ethical constraints, compose operation, transfer of information, question-based transfer and bi-directional transformation. It is now apparent that upgrader, update and write service functions of two-directional transformation invariably involve updating details and the application version schema of the RDB, or also that RDF is in R3 M, which is query driven and partially endorsed. Any additional conversion approach includes the required expertise, along with the improved flexibility and potential for upgrading, to accomplish bi-directional data transfer. Where there is a challenge in updating the switch that is published in RDF and RDB details, the key point in RDF is that this switch may be updated if the information is transferred to RDB, when RDB is transferred to RDF. This research operates in its way by merely adding a mapping function to the common intermediate category of knowledge collected by means of bidirectional data translation, as shown in Figure 50.

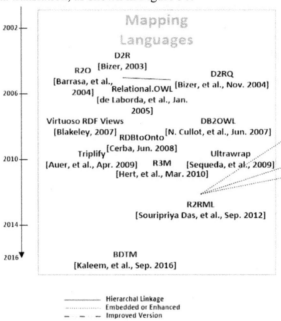

Figure 50: Comparison between different Tools, Techniques, and Languages

6.3 Implementation Tools

Java NetBeans 8.2 can also be used to access JDK 7 for Discovery Do the work. In NetBeans, packages of WordNet are deleted to use WordNet's technical resources for Synsets. 4.4 will be used for the intent of simplifying the multi agent's execution of JADE (Java Agent Creation Framework). Due to strong object-oriented speech features, stability and network resources, which are reliable and of course open to the public, Java-established technologies were chosen.

For institutions that produce Substantial information frameworks, Built-in development environments (IDEs) can be found from various actual programming providers. IDEs supply tools that are financing the item creation method, such as reviewers such as writing and changing endeavours and debuggers for uncovering motive blunders which produce software programs execute inaccurately. Main-stream IDEs integrate Eclipse (www.netbeans.org) and NetBeans (www.netbeans.org) as shown in Figure 51.

The Java API provides a Couple of Pre-defined data constructions, referred to as accumulations, used to put away parties of applicable content articles. These lessons provide effective methods that form outside, save, and retrieve your advice without even needing to find out of the way the information has been placed absent. It reduces the application-development period. You have used displays to save successions of articles or blog posts. Exhibits do not thus transform their dimension in implementation time for you to oblige more elements. The build-up category ArrayList (from package java.util) provides a beneficial answer with this particular dilemma. It could radically alter its measurement to accommodate greater parts.

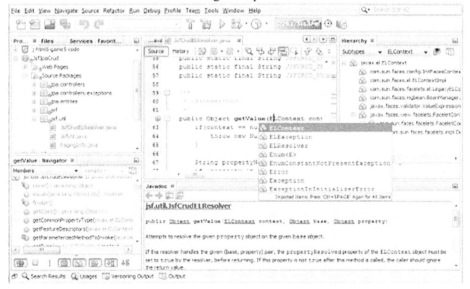

Figure 51: Snapshot of NetBeans

To display basic exemption Handling to look after processes, an exceptional scenario that transpires every time a strategy attempts to isolate a complete variety by zero. We provide a couple of classes in the maximal position of Java's exclusive scenario focusing on the class sequence. Since you are going to notice, only courses that extend Throwable (package java.lang) straightforwardly or from consequence might be used with exclusive instance care of. Then we attest to work with affixed exceptional scenarios. After you conjure an approach which shows that an exemption, then you can throw a different prosecution and string the initial someone towards the brand-new individual that lets you put in application-particular information towards this original distinctive scenario. We provide preconditions and postconditions that need to be true whenever your processes are all termed and should they come back, separately. We afterward pose announcements, that you simply may utilize in advance time and energy to purge your code. In this time, we have two brand new Java SE 7 exclusive instance focusing on components getting a variety of exemptions together with a grab handler along with also the brand new effort with-assets articulation that releases an advantage when it has employed as part of the effort sq. Course File that can be useful for regaining information about Records or registries out of the ring. Things, of course, Document do not open documents or Give any record managing talents. Be as It Could, Document protests have been Used as frequently as potential with items from additional java.io lessons to Determine files or catalogues to restrain.

6.4   How JADE1 works

It comprises a record of possessions as distinguished from the FIPA. A broker eager to convey something special should produce the following ACLMessage object, fulfil its properties together with suitable qualities, ultimately telephone the procedure sends out () implemented from the category Agent). Moreover, a broker eager to receive yourself a note should telephone get () or even blocking receive () methods, either actualized from the Agent course. Each of these traits of this ACLMessage merchandise might be obtained by way of this set/get () accessibility methods. All possessions are called following the titles of all these parameters, as distinguished from the FIPA. All those parameters whose kind will be the arrangement of traits, for example, beneficiary (for the event) might be obtained utilizing the plans include/getAll() at which the primary approach escalates the worth of this group. The next procedure supplies an Iterator more than each among many qualities at the group. Realize that most of the purchase processes come when the calibre has been set. What's more, this course likewise simplifies an arrangement of constants that should be used to revert into the FIPA performatives, i.e., urge, in-form, etc. Even though making still another ACL concept thing, these constants must be moved into the ACLMessage course constructor, having an objective to pick the material performative, as shown in Figure 52.

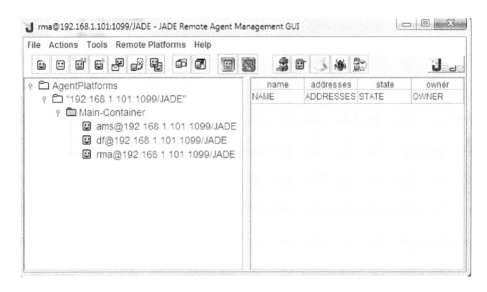

Figure 52: Snapshot of JADE

The reset () Tactic ignites the Estimations of most message areas. The toString() plan gives a String talking into this communication. This tactic should only be employed for monitoring functions. Backing to respond to an individual note, as signalled by FIPA details, a response must be formed taking into consideration an arrangement of most around framed fundamentals, as an instance, establishing the acceptable values for your credit score in-answer to, utilizing precisely the same debate identification, etc. JADE enables the program engineer in this mission with the plan createReply() of this ACLMessage course. This system gives another ACLMessage thing that's a significant solution for the one. At there, the applications engineer only must place up the application-specific open action and content material. A routine usage is harnessing to pass Java objects Between two brokers that the Java serialization. The ACLMessage course reinforces the applications engineer in this errand by allowing using Base64 monitoring throughout both methods setContentObject() and also getContentObject(). The broker undertakings. Implementing Agent methods, a broker Must possess the capability to execute a couple of murderous tasks at the light of varied occasions that are outside. The ending target to earn broker management successful, cach JADE (displayed in Figure 4-2) broker is created from the solitary implementation series, and each among its undertakings must be actualized as behavioural content. The engineer that would like to perform an agent-particular project should describe an individual or maybe more behaviour sub-classes, instantiate them, and insert the behaviour content articles to this broker mission checklist. Even the Agent course that ought to be extended out by representative computer software engineers also found two methods:

add behaviour (Behavior) and also remove behaviour, that empower to handle the geared-up undertaking's lineup of the certain broker. Notice that clinics and sub-practices might be contained in any given stage is demanded, and maybe not simply interior Agent.setup() strategy. Adding a behaviour should be considered a way to build a second (pleasant) implementation series within their broker.

Class Habits provides a theoretical foundation course into representative Practices, allowing behaviour reserving of its solid course. Additionally, it lays out the assumption for behaviour reserving since it requires Consideration condition moves (i.e., obstructing and re-starting that a behaviour item). This approach renders untouched Alternative techniques of a broker, together these traces allowing for better grained Get a handle on broker multi-tasking. This procedure sets the behaviour at a lineup of Obstructed clinics and creates impact if movement () yields). Every obstructed behaviour is re-scheduled if a second communication comes.

6.5 MySQL1

A database Will Be sorted Outside Buildup of advice. Additionally, there certainly is a large array of approaches for sorting out advice to boost simple control and access. A database administration platform (DBMS) presents elements to setting off, sorting outside, regaining, and shifting advice for several customers. Database administration techniques simply take into account the entry and ability of advice minus empathy regarding the inner representation of advice. Now's most popular database methods are all relational databases. A dialect named SQL supposed "spin-off," as its unique letters would be that the common global dialect employed around with relational databases to do issues (i.e., to require information that satisfies specified standards) also to restrain facts. [Notice: Since you discover out about SQL," you are going to observe some authors writing "that a SQL articulation" (that take on that the elocution "spinoff") as well as many others writing "a SQL excuse" (which trust the respective letters have been taken care of). In this novel, we emphasize SQL as "sequel."] The JDK currently conveys an undercover Java RDBMS referred to as Java DB Oracles' type of Apache Derby as shown in Figure 53.

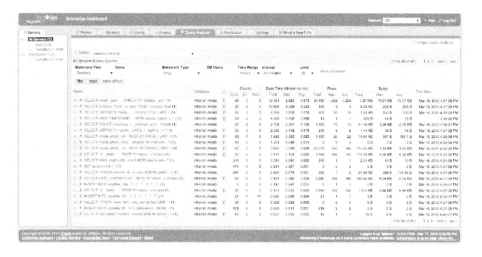

Figure 53: Snapshot of MySQL

6.6 Conclusion

Advice is Becoming stored and presented with distinct data units onto the broad scale, because of the, emerging details using various data designs and types reduce databases and devices potential to organize for facts analysis due to diminished data resemblance. A key part, to not be dismissed, is the fact that a notable region of the technique is taking a snapshot of customary databases and devices. Change from the info, procedure, and getting ready versions are poised to be more dedicated to beating these pesky problems by embracing data conversion mechanics. But these remedies tend not to insure to overcome issues associated with eloquent use of information conversion attributes. It attracts they should think of bidirectional data conversion methodology using a mutual terminology for information representation to overcome dilemmas of an upgrade regarding information and metadata.

7   EMERGING RESEARCH

The Colossal increment at the Amount and many-sided Caliber of Accessible data about the net attracted about a more the most effective interest in systems and instruments which may manage advice semantically. The ebb and leak training in information retrieval generally count about the watchword-based query over full-message info, and it is exhibited with a bag-of-words. About the flip side, this kind of version overlooks the real data in articles. For controlling this issue, ontologies are suggested for comprehension representation, and which can be such days that the base of semantic net software. The two-information extraction and retrieval procedures might benefit from these kinds of metadata, that supplies semantics to content that is plain.

7.1   Understanding Different Concepts

7.1.1   Extensible Markup Language (XML) and Schema

XML (DTD-Document Style Performance in summary), a subsection of all An XML routine dialect of this within a substantial period length and can be on the best way to thrive till XML Schema, in the past, come (Bray, Paoli, Sperberg-McQueen, Maler, and Yergeau, 1998). Its restricted capacities compared together with additional mapping dialects. Its main developing square consists of an element and a characteristic. This existing simple truth is generally spoken with using varied interlocking part constructions.

XML Schema has been a continuing effort of W3C to simply help and, at the lengthy-term, supplant DTD from the XML planet. XML Schema intends to become expressive than DTD and additional usable using way of a wider variety of utilizations. It's many different publication approaches, as an instance, an inheritance to get elements and attributes, consumer distinguished datatypes.

7.1.2   WordNet

WordNet has a substantial lexical established Database for speaking English. Modifiers, verbs, nouns, along with intensifiers, are assembled to collections of abstract synonyms referred to in addition to Synsets, just about every inter-connecting an off-beat understanding. Synsets are collections of English phrases that can be formed collection/Establish of synonyms. Synsets have inter-woven by way of a method of computing lexical and semantic institutions. The achievement scheme of related phrases and theories are available with this app. Additionally, WordNet is completely and publicly reachable when planning on carrying. The Procedure Is revealed in Figure 54.

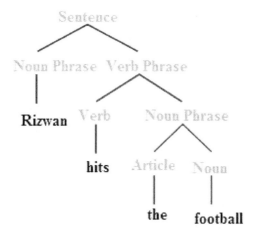

Figure 54: Basics Sentence structure in WordNet (Synsets)

The bulk of links of WordNet merge phrases with the very same grammar function (POS). WordNet is composed thus of four subnetworks, with a couple of Cross-POS tips, one each for words, verbs, descriptors and intensifiers. The 'morphosemantic' Cross-POS relations unites Keep a seminally similar sentence to take a turn towards G.WordNet being pictorial, as shown in Figure 55.

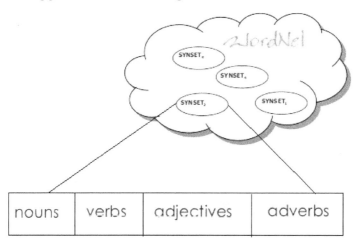

Figure 55: SYNSET in WordNet

7.1.3 Semantic Web

The Internet is Currently Stirring Being a Collecting Of pages into a buildup of guidelines that performs on the Web. The very first go on for the interoperation while in the field of distinct instructions that may help in understanding to get a problem. In this research, found a section of world wide web companies should be based around the foundations of significance equivalence in between a critical representation of this leadership attendance looked after, and a depiction of this leadership reverted through advertising. In any case, by way of analysis theory, this match is beyond the representation abilities of registries, as an instance, UDDI and dialects, as an instance, WSDL.

7.1.4 Resource Description Framework (RDF)

Asserting an RDF (Resource Description Framework) triple utters that an institution, given with all the predicate, adopts one of the tools might be symbolized that a blend of subject and object. Such announcement agreeing with an RDF triple turned into an RDF announcement. Even a predicate for being a resource that will be looked at being a binary term can be an IRI and symbolizes a land, i.e., terms that include less than just two entities to become deducted from RDF kind. Semantic Internet, all those efforts towards enlarging the retrieval implementation, whereas shielding the simplicity of usage is going to ultimately get into the center of this subject of improving semantic searching with catchphrase centered ports. It is a testing errand since it needs elaborate questions to become answered with only a couple of watchwords. In any case, it should enable the triggered advice to become retrieved easily and provide a placement program to signify semantics and ontology considerably, as shown in Figure 56.

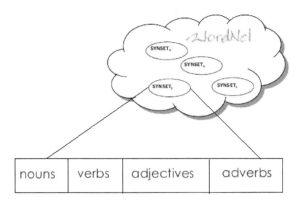

Figure 56: RDF Graph Example

7.1.5 NLP and Multi-Agents

Pc software Agents perform a critical function to receive competed in NLP and donate into the telltale cloud. A broker or person application existing at some type of computer is currently an application representative (subprogram or individual). To using the assistance of broker application, an arrangement is consequent between apps to use for many others. Inference of identical type indicates the capability to opt for action most useful appropriate and related. Various kinds of brokers as shown in Figure 57 comprise smart brokers (exclusively discovering a portion of artificial brain-power, as an instance, mastering and believing), self-ruling brokers, hauled representatives (staying implemented physically particular PCs), multi-agent frameworks (disseminated brokers which do not possess the talents to reach that target independently and within this way needs to impart), and more adaptive (brokers who may migrate their implementation onto identifying processors).

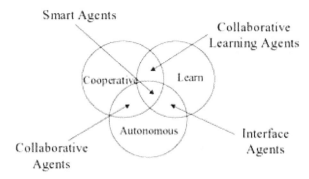

Figure 57: Types of Agents

7.1.6 Ontology

Ontology has become a vital Outlook in a lot of software to offer a semantic arrangement to expertise administration. Metaphysics can be an arrangement of the significance of chemical special understanding representation primitives (categories, connections, abilities, and constants). Ontology discusses this assorted levelled sub-categorizing to coordinate of comprehension regarding matters as indicated with their fundamental attributes.

The Huge Purpose of Taste. Metaphysics isn't in getting ready but instead in discussing relevance, evolution, and regeneration of pockets and, therefore, for enhancing the estimated comprehension market. An ontology may comprise data within a pre-determined critical dialect, but it may additionally comprise unstructured or unformalized information hauled into a feature dialect or perhaps a procedural text.

113

7.1.7 Problem Statement

Nowadays, NLP-based software faces difficulties after it Comes towards translation. They should overcome this issue; a broker will be skilled on special domain names to encourage far better consequences such as translation. What's more, there's just a significant requirement of punctuation for solving paragraph understanding if useful for rationale beneath artificial brains. In this, ontologies may play with a central role while they've got capacities of information linkage. This exploration task will aid in fixing an agent-based strategy to catch all potential connections built to get an English announcement, Lexicon. Using the aid of those Lexicons, we'd competent to change it into a mobile XML format and encouraged with lots of frameworks. RDF triple transformation is followed closely by XML which will be put to use as a useful resource for ontology production.

7.1.8 Research Objectives

A number of NLP methods are in operation. Diverse systems also introduced all-natural language processing methods on the market, likely for XML, RDF and narrative cloud output. In addition, artificial intelligence is used to efficiently interpret natural language. The professional activities around pure language production are the considerations contributing to this analysis. In an input signal and with the aid of WordNet Synsets, our creative assistance/app would definitely require herbal terminology. The XML and RDF are immediately turned on with multi-agents. Agent will talk and function as collective representatives with each other. XML and RDF would eventually soon take the form of a triple subject, Entity, and Prediate. The outcomes would depend on assumptions defined by the w3c.

7.1.9 Conclusion

Production of generic representations of Information and metadata Utilizing RDB, XML, and RDF. Information unit's Bi-directional information conversion methodology together with shared Language information representation to overcome dilemmas of upgrade regarding information and metadata. About the foundations of Bi-directional Data Growing Compatibility in information storage and recovery amongst RDB and SW was improved, as shown in Figure 58.

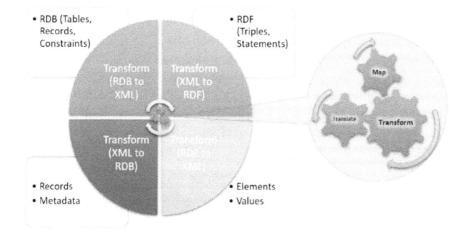

Figure 58 Production of generic representations of Information and metadata Utilizing RDB, XML, and RDF information units Bi-directional

7.1.10 Future work

- An example of research to execute and Manage the Shift
- BDTM to operate for many Form of RDBs
- We are boosting the Product to operate with Heterogeneous Information Versions, e.g., No SQL, OODB, etc.

7.1.11 Findings

- Handling Modify from RDB and RDF completely is potential
- Conventional data-oriented methods may operate together Side Intelligence established Techniques
- A more Frequent platform may enhance the compatibility of programs Work and coordinate collectively
- Data in the Shape of XML Can Readily Be reused in additional Software
- Same information via Other resources could be contrasted Common representation
- Updating information Won't Be an Issue anymore

8 OPPORTUNITIES

You will notice a slow progressing (and terminology and telltale) from routinely comprehensible lexicons into the lexical foundations and then to lexical ontologies in computational lexicology (a division of computational etymology). A decipherable lexicon speaks of the term paper and applies to details in digital form, such that the information can be answered on a virtual device. Even the basis for lexical searching in a coherent lexicon is different from the method since the term impacts are seen and relationships with opposing implications are indicated which enable for logical inference to be used for this advice.

8.1 Semantic Web vs Simple Web

A Semantic Network description begins with the semantic character. Semantic means important meaning. Relevance makes even meaningful usage of simple knowledge. Many data sources also have little meaning and need consumers to have it or complex programming concepts. Website sites, for instance, are filled with details and associated marks. The increased area of these tags is associated with providing instructions to display an entity. Semantically, we recognize that words surrounded by labels are still an accumulation of paragraphs using exactly the exact association using the per-user than additional material because of the importance of <p>. Some web pages consist of key semantics for worldwide web indicators utilizing <META> the label; in any situation, they have only segregated catchphrases and want linkages to provide an even more crucial setting. These semantics are frail and limit pursuits to correct matches. Primarily, databases comprise details and restricted semantic clues, if most of around termed tables and sections encircle the information.

Semantics provide a catchphrase image of beneficial importance through the build-up links. For instance, a standalone catchphrase, by way of example, the building exists on a web page specializing in ontologies. The label encircles the building watchword to show its significance clearly. Whatever the case, does construction mean growing an ontology or ontologies that interest on construction structures? The clumsiness of the past sentence takes focus to this trouble in sim deal with communication semantics in English. Semantics are left to get the individual per-user to decipher. So, assembling identifies with diverse watchwords, by way of instance, planner, building arranges, construction site, et cetera--that the relations uncover semantics. In case a proper benchmark grabs the game program of terms, the terms have quick to ascertained linguistic use policies. It is stunningly better if the terms themselves contour that a received benchmark or dialect. As this logical website of sentence arrangement tenets and dialect conditions grows through links, the semantics are further progressed.

The Semantic Web is sort of a rich internet of information depicted and joined using techniques to set up settings or semantics that carry fast to distinguished sentence arrangement and dialect assembles. Automatically, your application may contain semantics through programming guidelines; make certain that as it can, there isn't any formal standard for this tailored semantics. Moreover, sharing, accumulation, and acceptance are broadly speaking troublesome or unrealistic. Even the semantics are dropped in a labyrinth of if/else programming articulations, database lookups, and numerous other programming methods. It causes it to be hard to use this abundant data or also to remember everything. Even the nonstandard, sprinkled way of automatic semantic capture puts limits about it and makes it superfluously thoughts overpowering, essentially jumbled. Remaining lone, the importance of unique provisions; as an example, the building is simply discarded, as shown in Table 22.

Table 22: Comparison between Simple Web and Semantic Web

Elements	Simple Web	Semantic Web
Central Component	Semi-structured	Related data components
User	Humans	Machine
Linkage	Location-based	Location and Semantic-based
Vocabulary	Formatting	Meaning and Logics

8.2 Relational DB vs RDF

In Table 23, It's sh that the relational database depends upon a blueprint, such as an arrangement. At the same time, an RDF is based on semantic cloud-based declarations to prepare the construction. Relational databases are all restricted to a form of dating, the international secret. Even the Semantic Internet provides multi-dimensional relations, as an instance, can be a correlated together part of, and lots of other styles, including limitations, and sophistication, and plausible relations. In relational databases, for example, a desk or discipline can be wholly hard by containing a listing. RDF genuinely have zero parallel from how the persistent proclamations describe the arrangement or outline of their knowledge base as well as additionally, examples or people.

Connected Data Sets today comprise A profitable base finding out for encouraging analysis and regeneration aims throughout apps, recommenders, and exploratory pursuit frameworks especially. Now there's a requirement to simply take a gander in the achievements and inclinations in this fast-creating subject remembering the ending target to arrange the upcoming mining mechanics. The Resource Description Length (RDF) can be a dialect for talking with data concerning resources from the www. This Primer is likely to provide the per-user with the critical learning necessary to employ

RDF viably. It poses both the critical thoughts of RDF and defines its XML paragraph arrangement. It summarizes the way exactly to describe RDF vocabularies employing the RDF Vocabulary Description Language and supplies a record of several hauled RDF software.

Table 23: Comparison between the Relational Database and RDF

Feature	Relational database	Knowledgebase RDF
Structure	Schema	RDF Schema
Data	Rows	Instance statements
Administration language	DDL	Ontology statements
Query language	SQL	SPARQL
Relationships	Foreign keys	Multidimensional
Logic	External of database/triggers	Formal logic statements
Uniqueness	Key for table	URI

8.3 Integration of Lexical and Semantic data

Lexical metaphysics includes structured data regarding the phrases. It comprises telltale relations between your consequences of phrases (McCrae About the Flip Side, a Significant little bit of attached ontologies is assembled to get a specific division of Knowledge together with all the indication of connections between your thoughts of corresponding selection. This Moment, in almost any scenario, It's the insufficient Dimensions of dictionaries, thesauri, and ontologies that stand for a great dilemma for your applying. Then, widely of Use lexical metaphysics Comprises structured data regarding semantic and words connections. At the Interim, there Is no link to some division of comprehension. WordNet is seen as a Stand-out one of the most useful ventures with the sort, as shown in Figure 59.

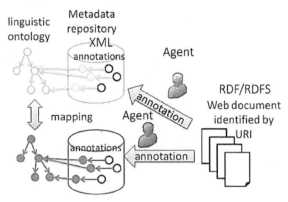

Figure 59: Annotation Methodology

To support advanced lexical characteristics via ontologies being a reference for Natural Language Processing (NLP) software.

8.4 Need for Multi-Task Learning

With all the expanding excitement for hauled and data equipment learning, then it's basic to produce frameworks that could simply take multiple, successive tasks following a moment; point. The idea of sharing information in between responsibilities to boost aggregate implementation was concentrated extensively by a whole lot multi-task finding out (MTL) perspective, at which project versions are willing all of them though. Overdue job in online MTL has revealed it is possible to find out jobs caked and reach roughly equal exactness into clump MTL while radically decreasing the computational expenditure. These abilities are all critical towards the progress of long-term learning methods that collect and continuously enhance knowledge about various endeavours within a life of encounter.

For inspiring data exchange in between action versions, one ordinary strategy employed by MTL calculations would always be to master and maintain up a frequent retail store of static model components; just about every endeavour version is subsequently granted as a homogenous mix of those sections. Some latest MTL patterns can employ this tactic, for example, different group calculations and the on the web accredited Lifelong Learning Algorithm (ELLA). In bunch MTL calculations, the stationary components are discovered at an identical time frame with all the project versions within a high-priced joint streamlining.

In recent research, cosmology linked notions happen to be caused by FIPA ACL articles dialect to manoeuvre data targeted toward operator's correspondence. But these will work possess only joined cosmology centered advice representation from correspondence material and from then on demonstrated that the upside-d of this association. In all honesty, regardless of the simple fact cosmology can talk to telltale effects demanded decidable pondering reinforce, it doesn't have any tool for characterizing intricate principle assembled cases to strengthen deduction. To discourse, this problem is by establishing a vibrating frame to add Semantic Internet creations to the ACL content compound. This base characterizes double identifying semantic buildings: the three-level finding out representation process such as Multi-layer Ontology Architecture and material content to get chemical dialect. The prior will be created by taking care of Semantic Web pile to reinforce doctrine constructed believing and guide established derivation. Constructing a lightweight Ontology-based content-language (LOCAL) to portray experts correspondence computer system interpretable manner Jena reasoner is employed as part of an email and application in an unambiguous, circumstance which experiences operators correspondence using

LOCAL as chemical dialect, OWL as doctrine dialect, along with SWRL as basic principle dialect to reveal the chance of this projected frame.

8.5 Multi-Agent System

The Preparation and Method of the Multi-agent established technique (MAS), at which self-agents form teams using various representatives for caring for problems, represent complicated undertakings that may prove to become much tougher when representative's work-in fresh, intelligent conditions, as an instance, the Semantic net. Remembering the ending target to deal with the intricacies of preparation and actualizing a MAS, domain-specific speech (DSL) as properly used indoors for MAS's advancement cycle.

Still another informed meeting area Frame named EasyMeeting investigates using multi-agent frameworks, Semantic Web ontologies, justification, and revelatory structures for protection and security. Expanding to an earlier pervasive processing frame, EasyMeeting presents crucial administrations and information into fulfilling individuals in perspective in their multi-faceted needs. The frame likewise abuses the atmosphere mindful financing provided from the Context Broker Architecture (Cobra). Cobra's savvy agent retains a standard placing design for many enrolling materials in the distance, along with upholds client defined protection agreements.

The Web-services world contains all inexactly combined dispersed frameworks that conform to fluctuations by using government portrayals that enable infantry, astute administration regulation, and reuse. Now, these government depictions are semantically destroyed, staying concerned with imitating the helpful markers of their administrations rather than describing their significance. None the less, used methodology (DAML) doesn't isolate the region unbiased, the insightful goal of the material (believed so considerably as discourse behaves) out of the special distance material, akin to equal breakthroughs from your multi-specialists' frameworks team.

We depict our experiences of Assessing and constructing an ontologically propelled web-services frame for Situational mindfulness and information triage at a mimicked compassionate guidebook Specific situation. Specifically, we Inspect the Advantages of using approaches from That the multi-specialists' frameworks set for isolating the willful strength of Messages out of their stuff, and also the use of those procedures within their in of the DAML Services model.

8.6 Natural Language, Ontology and Semantic Web

Nearly all the all-natural language ports only pay attention to a sure region of the concern (e.g., a port to your societal network, or even a port into an ontology). But in the view of customers, it will not produce a huge difference where in fact, the data has been placed off, but they basically ought to receive precisely the data within an integrated, uncomplicated, successful, successful, and fantastic method. So, to manage this problem, a non-special multi-operators conversational design and style which chooses after the breakup and overcome notion and believes just two different forms of pros. Professional operators have needed technical expertise in accessing to several information resources, and pick specialists organize them to offer a solid last reaction to this customer.

Distributed information over the Semantic internet utilizing ordinary agreements enables advice to become attached jointly, reused, and incorporated. Remembering the ending purpose to entirely help determine the capacity for reusing; therefore, regarding interlink information active diagrams, an intuitive way of questionnaire present utilization of RDF sayings is all demanded. Adding a frame to enable a customer to find exactly the absolute most as usually as potential travelling courses and namespaces within a grand Semantic Internet dataset, and also the basic principle connection layouts which exist one of these.

8.7 Sentence Structure Parsing

The paper depicts an approach for eliminating written addiction examinations of Language arrangements such as saying paragraphs parses. Possessing special deciding aim to detect normal actions in corpus communications that are crucial in accredited software, many NP family members are revised to the matching approach of syntactic family members utilized. By analyzing of the platform together with Mini-bar and the Hyperlink analyzer. The written dependence abstraction depicted this will be found from the Stanford Parser, obtainable on the market.

Even the Stanford composed environment depiction was suggested to supply significant depiction of those syntactic institutions at a sentence which may, without doubt, be appropriately blindsided by individuals devoid of etymological capability who must get rid of families that were printed. In contrast to the expression arrangement examples which have after a lengthy period ago in the phonetic collecting, it defines with institutions one of each sentence systematically as written dependency connected classes. Standard representation is quite readily available to non-language experts believing assignments, for example, information extraction out of material and so is successful about management software.

8.8 Transformation RDB, XML and RDF

XML (extensible Markup Language) Is little by little recognized while the norm for the representation of advice job from the area of Web. Founded following XML are offered with the home RDB sellers while in the industry sector while the improver or holder into the societal network regulating frame. Combo of this database, along with the XML database, contains information gleaned and schema. The paper supplies the doctrine of translating the theoretical structural representation of the relational database compacted into XML schema utilizing the EER (prolonged entity partnership) version. Information can subsequently farther manufacture a construal of the relational table to some XML archive file.

Much work Was performed in creating an Interpretation of societal networking to XML information devoid of consideration of advice demands partitioning. Every one of the moments, they are inclined to decode only a few tables descending right in an XML listing. They are employing DOM and De Normalization to your job with improved adaptability along with the imperatives market. This deformalizing schema into joint connections farther shifted into DOMs and then organized to an XML account shrub. Such advice states constraints located from the social interactions are awarded into an Element and Sub-component one of XML archives. The client selects an XML archive for every single, separated XML listing to your necessities. The process supplies adaptability into this customer to improve past a view of their societal database right into an XML report. The upcoming advancement of the paper would always be to make use of the stored information states to recover the very first societal network by your deciphered XML archives to get advice commerce about the information roadway.

Was broadly employed while the most inclusive settings for spread and buying and selling advice from globally Internet, as a result, its capability to bolster adaptive representations of advice. For the importance of shifting additional information components, as an instance, Object-Oriented Database (OODB) and Relational Database into XML, has enlarged. The goal with the paper would be to include some skilful strategy to modify OODB into XML, which may be used through a thorough number of end-clients who usually do not will need to function government. Regardless of how the paper indicates no publication methodology, nonetheless, it's focused on creating principle established doctrine to change-over OODB blueprint to XML diagram.

Certainly, one of those promises of Semantic Web software would always be to manage additional information. As the Extensible Markup Language (XML) has proven to become widely embraced being an almost universal transaction design such as advice, alongside shift dialects Such as XSLT and XQuery to decode in 1 XML set to a second, the next Source Description Framework (RDF) has finished up yet another Famous benchmark For facts representation and transaction, preserved with its very competent question Dialect SPARQL, which enables change and extraction of all RDF details. The ability to get the job done well with your two dialects by using a normal system One of the small numbers of useless measures which can be of today fundamental taking Care of the settings near each other. In This report, we reveal the XSPARQL dialect that, by linking XQuery along with SPARQL, enables us to question XML and RDF Facts using Precisely the Same method and, separately change one arrangement in one other. We focus on the Semantics with the merged dialect and pose the implementation, for example, discussion.

8.9   RDF Graph

PGV consists of 2 fundamental pieces: a) that the "PGV wayfarer" and b) that the "RDF pager" module with BRAHMS, our e-lite chief memory RDF stock-piling frame. Perhaps not like present graph representation approaches which project to reveal the entire diagram and immediately after that sift via unessential info, PGV commences using just a tiny bit of diagram and supplies the tools to investigate and picture pertinent advice about large RDF ontologies. We implemented a couple of approaches to assume and explore troublesome areas from the diagram, i.e., hubs together with expansive amounts of instantaneous neighbors. Considering their client commanded the semantics-driven path of this analysis, the PGV voyager gets the essential sub-diagrams in your RDF pager and enables their incremental representation to deny the laid sub-charts in-place. We design the Dilemma of imagining large RDF data places analyze our port along with its use, and through a Managed analysis, we show the Benefits of PGV.

REFERENCES

ALBAHAR, B. & HUANG, J.-B. Guided image-to-image translation with bi-directional feature transformation. Proceedings of the IEEE International Conference on Computer Vision, 2019. 9016-9025.

ALDABBAS, H., BAJAHZAR, A., ALRUILY, M., QURESHI, A. A., LATIF, R. M. A. & FARHAN, M. 2020. Google Play Content Scraping and Knowledge Engineering using Natural Language Processing Techniques with the Analysis of User Reviews. *Journal of Intelligent Systems,* 30, 192-208.

ALOUFI, K., MALIK, K., NAEEM, T. & MIR, R. 2019. Data Transmission and Capacity over Efficient IoT Energy Consumption. *IJCSNS,* 19, 102.

ANDERSEN, M., MICHEL, L., ROECKER, C. & SCARTEZZINI, J.-L. 2001. Experimental assessment of bi-directional transmission distribution functions using digital imaging techniques. *Energy and Buildings,* 33, 417-431.

ANDERSEN, M., RUBIN, M., POWLES, R. & SCARTEZZINI, J.-L. 2005. Bi-directional transmission properties of Venetian blinds: experimental assessment compared to ray-tracing calculations. *Solar Energy,* 78, 187-198.

BINDU, N., SANKAR, C. P. & KUMAR, K. S. 2019. From conventional governance to e-democracy: Tracing the evolution of e-governance research trends using network analysis tools. *Government Information Quarterly,* 36, 385-399.

BLUE, V. J. & ADLER, J. L. 2001. Cellular automata microsimulation for modeling bi-directional pedestrian walkways. *Transportation Research Part B: Methodological,* 35, 293-312.

CALLOW, G. & KALAWSKY, R. 2013. A Satisficing Bi-Directional Model Transformation Engine using Mixed Integer Linear Programming. *J. Object Technol.,* 12, 1:1-43.

EBERT, P. S. 2006. Bi-directional data flow in a real time tracking system. Google Patents.

FARHAN, H. N., BUKHARI, S. S. H. & MALIK, K. R. An E-Assessment Methodology Based on Artificial Intelligence Techniques to Determine Students' Language Quality and Programming Assignments' Plagiarism Farhan Ullah1, 4, Abdullah Bajahzar2, Hamza Aldabbas3, Muhammad.

FOSTER, J. N., GREENWALD, M. B., MOORE, J. T., PIERCE, B. C. & SCHMITT, A. 2005. Combinators for bi-directional tree transformations: a linguistic approach to the view update problem. *ACM SIGPLAN Notices,* 40, 233-246.

HONGWEI, S., SHUSHENG, Z., JINGTAO, Z. & JING, W. 2003. Three-Tier Bi-Directional Data Integration between XML (eXtensible Markup Language) and RDB (Relational Data Base). *JOURNAL-NORTHWESTERN POLYTECHNICAL UNIVERSITY,* 21, 514-517.

IFTIKHAR, N. & PEDERSEN, T. B. 2011. Flexible exchange of farming device data. *Computers and Electronics in Agriculture,* 75, 52-63.

JHANJHI, N., BROHI, S. N. & MALIK, N. A. Proposing a Rank and Wormhole Attack Detection Framework using Machine Learning. 2019 13th International Conference on Mathematics, Actuarial Science, Computer Science and Statistics (MACS), 2019. IEEE, 1-9.

KOK, S., ABDULLAH, A., JHANJHI, N. & SUPRAMANIAM, M. 2019. Prevention of crypto-ransomware using a pre-encryption detection algorithm. *Computers,* 8, 79.

KOTOB, A. Z. 1987. Transforming computations with bi-directional data flow into ones with uni-directional data flow on linear systolic arrays. North Carolina State University. Center for Communications and Signal Processing.

LATIF, R. M. A., ABDULLAH, M. T., SHAH, S. U. A., FARHAN, M., IJAZ, F. & KARIM, A. Data Scraping from Google Play Store and Visualization of its Content for Analytics. 2019 2nd International Conference on Computing, Mathematics and Engineering Technologies (iCoMET), 2019a. IEEE, 1-8.

LATIF, R. M. A., BELHAOUARI, S. B., SAEED, S., IMRAN, L. B., SADIQ, M. & FARHAN, M. 2020. Integration of Google Play Content and Frost Prediction Using CNN: Scalable IoT Framework for Big Data. *IEEE Access,* 8, 6890-6900.

LATIF, R. M. A., FARHAN, M., FARAH IJAZ, M. U. & SHAH, S. U. A. 2019b. A SMART METHODOLOGY FOR ANALYZING CHRONIC KIDNEY DISEASE DETECTION. *Journal of Natural and Applied Sciences Pakistan,* 1, 206-216.

LATIF, R. M. A., UMER, M., TARIQ, T., FARHAN, M., RIZWAN, O. & ALI, G. A Smart Methodology for Analyzing Secure E-Banking and E-Commerce Websites. 2019 16th International Bhurban Conference on Applied Sciences and Technology (IBCAST), 2019c. IEEE, 589-596.

LOPRINZI, P. D., HEROD, S. M., CARDINAL, B. J. & NOAKES, T. D. 2013. Physical activity and the brain: a review of this dynamic, bi-directional relationship. *Brain Research,* 1539, 95-104.

MAAMARI, F., ANDERSEN, M., DE BOER, J., CARROLL, W. L., DUMORTIER, D. & GREENUP, P. 2006. Experimental validation of simulation methods for bi-directional transmission properties at the daylighting performance level. *Energy and Buildings,* 38, 878-889.

MALIK, K. R., FARHAN, M., HABIB, M. A., KHALID, S., AHMAD, M. & GHAFIR, I. 2018a. Remote access capability embedded in linked data using bi-directional transformation: Issues and simulation. *Sustainable cities and society,* 38, 662-674.

MALIK, K. R., KHAN, I. I., ALOUFI, K. S., CHOUIKHI, N. & HUSSAIN, A. 2020. Semantic Interoperability for Context-Aware Autonomous Control using IoT and Edge Computing.

MALIK, K. R., SAM, Y., HUSSAIN, M. & ABUARQOUB, A. 2018b. A methodology for real-time data sustainability in smart city: Towards inferencing and analytics for big-data. *Sustainable Cities and Society,* 39, 548-556.

MCBRIEN, P. & POULOVASSILIS, A. Data integration by bi-directional schema transformation rules. Proceedings 19th International Conference on Data Engineering (Cat. No. 03CH37405), 2003. IEEE, 227-238.

OKUNSEINDE, F. & STADING, T. 2010. Bi-directional data mapping tool. Google Patents.

PON, L.-S., SUN, M. & SCLABASSI, R. J. The bi-directional spike detection in EEG using mathematical morphology and wavelet transform. 6th International Conference on Signal Processing, 2002., 2002. IEEE, 1512-1515.

RAMZAN, M., AWAN, S. M., ALDABBAS, H., ABID, A., FARHAN, M., KHALID, S. & LATIF, R. M. A. 2019. Internet of medical things for smart D3S to enable road safety. *International Journal of Distributed Sensor Networks,* 15, 1550147719864883.

REN, A., LIANG, C., HYUG, I., BROH, S. & JHANJHI, N. 2020. A Three-Level Ransomware Detection and Prevention Mechanism. *EAI Endorsed Transactions on Energy Web,* 7.

ROUSE, A., STANSLASKI, S., CONG, P., JENSEN, R., AFSHAR, P., ULLESTAD, D., GUPTA, R., MOLNAR, G., MORAN, D. & DENISON, T. 2011. A chronic generalized bi-directional brain–machine interface. *Journal of neural engineering,* 8, 036018.

ROZIN, A. & KAPLUN, G. 1998. Capcitively coupled bi-directional data and power transmission system. Google Patents.

SABORNIE, E. J., KAUFFMAN, J. M., ELLIS, E. S., MARSHALL, K. J. & ELKSNIN, L. K. 1988. BI-DIRECTIONAL AND CROSS-CATEGRICAL SOCIAL STATUS OF LEARNING DISABLED, BEHAVIORALLY DISORDERED, AND NONHANDICAPPED ADOLESCENTS. *The Journal of Special Education,* 21, 39-56.

SAEED, S., ABDULLAH, A. & JHANJHI, N. 2019. Analysis of the lung cancer patient's for data mining tool. *IJCSNS,* 19, 90.

SAEED, S., JHANJHI, N., NAQVI, M., HUMAYUN, M. & PONNUSAMY, V. 2020a. Analyzing the Performance and Efficiency of IT-Compliant Audit Module Using Clustering Methods. *Industrial Internet of Things and Cyber-Physical Systems: Transforming the Conventional to Digital.* IGI Global.

SAEED, S., JHANJHI, N., NAQVI, M., PONNUSAMY, V. & HUMAYUN, M. 2020b. Analysis of Climate Prediction and Climate Change in Pakistan Using Data Mining Techniques. *Industrial Internet of Things and Cyber-Physical Systems: Transforming the Conventional to Digital.* IGI Global.

SANGKARAN, T., ABDULLAH, A. & JHANJHI, N. 2020a. Criminal Community Detection Based on Isomorphic Subgraph Analytics. *Open Computer Science,* 10, 164-174.

SANGKARAN, T., ABDULLAH, A. & JHANJHI, N. 2020b. Criminal Network Community Detection Using Graphical Analytic Methods: A Survey. *EAI Endorsed Transactions on Energy Web,* 7.

SINGH, V., FOGELSONG, B., MARCUCCIO, S., CHAPMAN, C., PAUL, T. & BRANNIGAN, J. 2012. Real-time, bi-directional data management. Google Patents.

SINGHAL, V., JAIN, S., ANAND, D., SINGH, A., VERMA, S., RODRIGUES, J. J., JHANJHI, N. Z., GHOSH, U., JO, O. & IWENDI, C. 2020. Artificial Intelligence Enabled Road Vehicle-Train Collision Risk Assessment Framework for Unmanned Railway Level Crossings. *IEEE Access,* 8, 113790-113806.

126

STANSLASKI, S., CONG, P., CARLSON, D., SANTA, W., JENSEN, R., MOLNAR, G., MARKS, W. J., SHAFQUAT, A. & DENISON, T. An implantable bi-directional brain-machine interface system for chronic neuroprosthesis research. 2009 Annual International Conference of the IEEE Engineering in Medicine and Biology Society, 2009. IEEE, 5494-5497.

STEENKAMP, A. L. 2017. *Examining the Changing Role of Supervision in Doctoral Research Projects: Emerging Research and Opportunities: Emerging Research and Opportunities*, IGI Global.

TALLAT, R., LATIF, R. M. A., ALI, G., ZAHEER, A. N., FARHAN, M. & SHAH, S. U. A. Visualization and Analytics of Biological Data by Using Different Tools and Techniques. 2019 16th International Bhurban Conference on Applied Sciences and Technology (IBCAST), 2019. IEEE, 291-303.

USMANI, R. S. A., PILLAI, T. R., HASHEM, I. A. T., JHANJHI, N. & SAEED, A. 2020. A Spatial Feature Engineering Algorithm for Creating Air Pollution Health Datasets.

ZHAO, R., YAN, R., WANG, J. & MAO, K. 2017. Learning to monitor machine health with convolutional bi-directional LSTM networks. *Sensors,* 17, 273.

ZHOU, Y. & HO, S.-T. 2007. Integrated planar composite coupling structures for bi-directional light beam transformation between a small mode size waveguide and a large mode size waveguide. Google Patents.

Kaleem Razzaq Malik was born in Multan, Punjab, Pakistan in 1984. He received the M.S. degrees in computer science from the National University of Computer and Emerging Sciences, Lahore, PAK in 2008 and the Ph.D. degree in computer science from University of Engineering and Technology, Lahore, PAK, in 2018. He is now working as Associate Professor in Air University, Multan Campus, Multan, Pakistan from March 2018 - date performing duties like Teaching and Research. He has worked as Assistant Professor in COMSATS Institute of Information Technology, Sahiwal, Pakistan from December 2015 – March 2018 and as Lecturer in Department of Software Engineering, Government College University Faisalabad, Pakistan from June 2013 – November 2015 (2 year 5 months) performing duties like Teaching. He has also worked as instructor of computer science in Virtual University of Pakistan. University level more than 10 years of teaching experience. He has published various articles in eminent National and International Journals with more than 100 citations. He has performed the role of reviewer for many top ranking international well reputed SCIE Indexed Journals of Springer, IEEE and Elsevier. He has been member of technical program committee of International Conferences His interests include Bigdata, Cloud Computing, Data Sciences, and Semantic Web.

Dr. Muhammad Farhan is working as an Assistant Professor in the Department of Computer Science, COMSATS University Islamabad, Sahiwal Campus, Pakistan. He had worked as a Lecturer in the same department. He completed his Ph.D. in 2017 in the field of Computer Science from the Department of Computer Sciences and Engineering at the University of Engineering and Technology (UET), Pakistan. He obtained MSCS in 2010 from the University of Management and Technology (UMT), Pakistan. He has received BSCS in 2007 from Virtual University of Pakistan (VU). He also had worked as an Instructor of Computer Science at the Virtual University of Pakistan for about 5 years. He started his research career with the publication of a conference paper in San Luis Potosí, Mexico, IEEE CPS. He has honored for winning travel grant provided by ACM and Microsoft for the presentation of a student paper in the ACM/SIGAPP Symposium (Human-Computer Interaction track) held by the University of Salamanca, Spain. He has published a good number of SCI-indexed impact factor journal papers, which are published by Journal of Real-Time Image Processing by Springer, Multimedia Tools and Applications by Springer, International Journal of Distributed Sensor Networks by SAGE Journals, EURASIA Journal of Mathematics, Science and Technology

Education by MODESTUM, Life Science Journal by Marshland Press and in various renowned journals of IEEE, Springer, Elsevier and Hindawi. His interests include Data Science, machine & deep learning, and Internet of Things.

 Dr Noor Zaman Jhanjhi is currently working as Associate Professor with Taylor's University Malaysia. He has great international exposure in academia, research, administration, and academic quality accreditation. He worked with ILMA University, and King Faisal University (KFU) for a decade. He has 20 years of teaching & administrative experience. He has an intensive background of academic quality accreditation in higher education besides scientific research activities, he had worked a decade for academic accreditation and earned ABET accreditation twice for three programs at CCSIT, King Faisal University, Saudi Arabia. He also worked for National Commission for Academic Accreditation and Assessment (NCAAA), Education Evaluation Commission Higher Education Sector (EECHES) formerly NCAAA Saudi Arabia, for institutional level accreditation. He also worked for the National Computing Education Accreditation Council (NCEAC).

Dr Noor Zaman has awarded as top reviewer 1% globally by WoS/ISI (Publons) recently for the year 2019. He has edited/authored more than 13 research books with international reputed publishers, earned several research grants, and a great number of indexed research articles on his credit. He has supervised several postgraduate students, including master's and PhD. Dr Noor Zaman Jhanjhi is an Associate Editor of IEEE ACCESS, moderator of IEEE TechRxiv, Keynote speaker for several IEEE international conferences globally, External examiner/evaluator for PhD and masters for several universities, Guest editor of several reputed journals, member of the editorial board of several research journals, and active TPC member of reputed conferences around the globe.

RANA M. AMIR LATIF received the B.S.C.S. degree from COMSATS University Islamabad Sahiwal, Sahiwal, Pakistan. He is graduated in M.S. degree from COMSATS University Islamabad Sahiwal, Sahiwal, Pakistan. He is currently doing job as a Lecture in Barani Institute of Sciences, Sahiwal. He also had worked as a Lecture of Computer Science at the Quaid-e-Azam College of Engineering and Technology, Sahiwal for about one years. He is also a Research Assistant with the Department of Computer Science, CUI, under the supervision of Dr. M. Farhan. He has many research publications in high impact factor journals also he has many publications in well reputed international conferences. He is also doing a funded project with the government of Pakistan in national research program for universities. His research interests include machine learning, data sciences, and the IoT.

Prof. Dr. Khalid Hussain received his MS IT degree in 1996 from Preston University Islamabad. He did M.S. CS from COMSATS Institute of Information Technology Islamabad in 2007 specializing in Wireless Communication and Networks. He received his Ph.D. from Universiti Tecknolotgi Malaysia specializing Wireless Networks Security.

Syed Jawad Hussain completed his B.S. with major in Mathematics in 1999. He received the master's in computer science degree from International Islamic University, Islamabad, Pakistan in 2002. He worked in the industry for five years as embedded system developer. He did Postgraduate diploma from Massey University in 2009 and PhD in 2015 in computer networks. Currently working as Associate Professor in barani institute of information technology, BIIT, PMAS, Arid Agriculture University Rawalpindi. His Current research interest includes machine learning, e-Learning and cyber security.

Publisher: Eliva Press SRL

Email: info@elivapress.com